The Philosophy of Edith Stein

The Philosophy of Edith Stein

From Phenomenology to Metaphysics

METTE LEBECH

PETER LANG

Oxford · Bern · Berlin · Bruxelles · Frankfurt am Main · New York · Wien

Bibliographic information published by Die Deutsche Nationalbibliothek
Die Deutsche Nationalbibliothek lists this publication in the Deutsche Nationalbibliografie;
detailed bibliographic data is available on the Internet at http://dnb.d-nb.de.

A catalogue record for this book is available from the British Library.

Library of Congress Control Number: 2015934183

ISBN 978-3-0343-1851-8 (print)
ISBN 978-3-0353-0710-8 (eBook)

Cover image © Edith Stein Archiv, Karmel Maria vom Frieden.

© Peter Lang AG, International Academic Publishers, Bern 2015
Hochfeldstrasse 32, CH-3012 Bern, Switzerland
info@peterlang.com, www.peterlang.com, www.peterlang.net

This publication has been peer reviewed.

Contents

Acknowledgements

The material for this volume consists of previously published articles. All have been revised to fit them into this patchwork monograph, most of them substantially. Permission has been sought for reprinting or translating them. Thanks are due to Therese Meehan, Anna-Marie Lebech Sørensen and Liz Meade for careful reading of the chapters and many helpful suggestions.

Chapter 1 is based on a German version of the paper, originally given to the *Edith Stein Gesellschaft Deutschland* in Salzburg, 17 April 2010 and published in the *Edith Stein Jahrbuch*, 2011, pp. 71–86. It was subsequently given in a substantially revised English version as a paper in Centre of Dialogue and Prayer Oświęcim/Auschwitz to commemorate Stein's death, 8 June, 2012. The title of the paper was 'Edith Stein as a European Philosopher'. A German version of this paper is to be published with the other papers given at the conference by P. Manfred Deselaers.

Chapter 2 and 3 were originally printed in *The Yearbook of the Irish Philosophical Society*. A much shorter version of the first paper was given at the *Intercorporeality and Intersubjectivity International Conference*, UCD, 6–8 June 2008, which was published in *Maynooth Philosophical Papers*, 2008, ed. Simon Nolan, Maynooth, pp. 16–20 under the title 'Stein's Phenomenology of the Body. The Human Being between Description of Experience and Social Construction'. It was subsequently expanded for a longer paper given at the Centre for Subjectivity Research, University of Copenhagen 13 January 2009, and published in *The Yearbook of the Irish Philosophical Society*, 2008, ed. Fiachra Long, Maynooth, pp. 61–70. The second paper was first given in the Invited Speakers Series at Wheaton College, Illinois, 13 October 2009, and then at the Baltimore Carmel's *Festival of Learning*, Maryland, 14 November 2009. It was published in *The Yearbook of the Irish Philosophical Society*, 2010, ed. Julia Hynes, Maynooth, pp. 139–50 as 'Stein's Value Theory'.

Chapter 4 is based on 'Edith Stein's Value-Theory and its Importance for her Conception of the State' printed in *Europa und seine Anderen. Emmanuel Levinas, Edith Stein, Jozef Tischner*, ed. by Hanna-Barbara. Gerl-Falkovitz, René Kaufmann and Hans Rainer Sepp (Dresden: Thelem, 2010), pp. 145–54. The volume holds papers given at a conference in Dresden with the same title in June 2009.

Chapter 5 is a translation of 'Bildung des Menschen – Bildung Europas. Der Einfluss der Christitentum im Lichte der Philosophie Edith Steins', published in *Die Bildung Europas. Eine Topographie des Möglichen im Horizont der Freiheit*, ed. by Hanna-Barbara Gerl-Falkovitz, René Kaufmann and Hans Rainer Sepp (Dresden: Thelem, 2012), gathering papers from a conference held in Dresden in June 2010.

Chapter 6 is based on a paper originally given at Institute for Research in the Humanities, University of Wisconsin-Madison, Madison, Wisconsin, 21 October 2009, entitled 'The Constitution of Human Dignity according to Edith Stein'. It was developed for another paper given in the Newman House, UCD, 16 December 2013, as part of an EU funded project entitled 'Discovering the "We"' under the title 'The Constitution of Human Dignity according to the Phenomenology of Edith Stein'. It was given again in Mary Immaculate College, Limerick on the 8 February 2014. After a substantial revision, which owes a lot to the critical reading of Thomas Szanto, it is under consideration for publication by Springer in a volume edited by Dermot Moran and Thomas Szanto under the title 'Human Dignity according to Edith Stein'. A German version was given in Vienna 24 October 2014, under the title 'Menschenwürde im Lichte der Philosophie Edith Steins', at a conference organised by the *Edith Stein Gesellschaft Österreich*. It was also given at the Hochschule Heiligenkreuz in Heiligenkreuz, Austria, on the 25 October 2014, slightly altered, at a conference organised by the EUPHRat Institute entitled *Europa eine Seele geben*, under the title 'Europa und die Menschenwürde'. The first of the German papers will appear in the *Edith Stein Jahrbuch* 2015, and the second in the proceedings of the said conference.

Chapter 7 is based on an article entitled 'Edith Stein's Education Theory in *The Structure of the Human Person*', first printed in *REA, Religion, Education & the Arts*, Issue V: The Philosophy of Education, edited by

Ian Leask, 2005, pp. 55–70, and subsequently reprinted in *What Price the University? A Special Issue of the Maynooth Philosophical Papers*, ed. by Thomas Kelly, NUI Maynooth, 2006, pp. 163–78.

Chapter 8 originates as a paper given to the *Newman Society*, UCD, Ireland, 11 February 2009 commissioned to address the topic 'female identity' in the context of someone else speaking to the topic of 'male identity'. It was published under the title 'What can we learn from Edith Stein's Philosophy of Woman?' in the *Yearbook of the Irish Philosophical Society*, 2009, ed. Cyril McDonnell, Maynooth, pp. 215–24.

Chapter 9 is based on 'Edith Stein's Thomism', *Maynooth Philosophical Papers*, 2014, Issue 7, pp. 20–32. The first version of this paper was given at the Centre for Thomistic Studies at the University of St Thomas, Houston, Texas, 21 March 2013, and a subsequent version was given in Dublin, at a Cairde Tomáis Naofa conference 7 June 2014 in Ely University Centre.

Chapter 10 was published in *Phenomenology 2010. Traditions, Transitions and Challenges*, ed. Dermot Moran and Hans Rainer Sepp, OPO (Bucharest: Zeta Books, 2011), pp. 138–54, under the title 'Beginning to Read *Finite and Eternal Being*'. It was previously given at a conference of the Irish Philosophical Society in Maynooth, 4 April 2009.

Chapter 11 originated as a paper at the Newman Society, UCD, on 29 November 2006, entitled 'Edith Stein and Martin Heidegger'. It was rewritten for a Cairde Tomáis Naofa conference, in Maynooth, 10 March 2007 with the title 'Edith Stein and Martin Heidegger on the Meaning of Being'. It was expanded for a collection edited by Kathleen Haney to be published by ICS Publications.

Chapter 12 is based on 'The recognition of human dignity in the person living with dementia: reflections in the light of the phenomenology of Edith Stein' published in its English form in *An Irish Reader in Moral Theology. The Legacy of the Last 50 Years*, Vol. III: Medical and Bio Ethics, ed. by Enda McDonagh and Vincent MacNamara (Dublin: Columba Press, 2013), pp. 66–76. This English version is a translation of 'Die Anerkannung der Menschenwürde von Demenzkranken. Untersuchungen im Lichte der Philosophie Edith Steins' in *Leid und Mitleid bei Edith Stein*, ed. by Malgorzata Bogaczyk-Vormayr, Elisabeth Kapferer and Clemens Sedmak (Salzburg: Verlag Anton Pustet, 2013), pp. 136–48. Originally the paper was given in English at the IACB International Conference in Cardinal Schulte Haus, Cologne, Germany, 14 July 2009. This chapter is dedicated to Annette Bolhorn and her team, who expertly looked after my mother until she died at Dorte Marie Hjemmet, Rødovrevej, Copenhagen in 2007.

The book is supported by a grant from the National University of Ireland.

Glossary

To facilitate the reading of this book it is useful to define a few terms often used by Stein. These are meant for the reader to have recourse to throughout the reading of the book, whenever doubt arises about the meanings of the words. They are mostly related to the phenomenological method, which she develops, tests and perfects throughout her life.

A PRIORI AND ONTOLOGY

Eidetic variation is possible in imagination because essences are *a priori*, i.e. before (concrete) experience, and because one can gain insight into *a priori* relationships relatively independently of empirical experience. Thus I can discuss meaningfully what pertains to the essence of a dragon or to Sleeping Beauty, without either existing, or without me having seen either. Ontologies are sciences of essence in that they investigate various types of essence (e.g. nature, spirit).

CONSTITUTION AND CONSTITUTIONAL ANALYSIS

'Constitution' is a term Stein inherits from Husserl, who uses it systematically to mean the way in which things appear as one (for me, for us). Constitution happens quasi-automatically, but not without the involvement or activity of the 'I'. It is the primary activity of the 'I', its first expression, its function. Whenever there is constitution, there is an 'I' (or several 'I''s); whenever there is an I, it is because there is constitution. This is why 'I''s are constituted *as constituting*, according to Stein (and Husserl). Constitutional analysis is, alongside eidetic and ontic analysis, a type of phenomenological analysis practiced by the phenomenologists. It attempts to establish how the unity of some object comes about for me or for us, i.e. in what acts it is identified or constituted as one.

EIDOS AND EIDETIC ANALYSIS

Eidetic analysis, which is complementary to constitutional analysis, investigates the *eidos* or essence of something, i.e. what something is. It does that in particular by means of *eidetic variation*, the method according to which the essence of something is varied in imagination until it no longer is that thing.

EMPATHY

Empathy is the experience of foreign experience, or the act in which foreign experience is experienced. Empathy is necessary for me to gain an objective view of myself, and constitute myself as a psycho-physical person in the world.

INTER-SUBJECTIVE CONSTITUTION

Inter-subjective constitution is social construction resulting from the constitution of many individuals constituting each other as forming part of a complex network of relations.

METAPHYSICS

In contrast with ontology metaphysics concerns the existing world, not merely its essential structure. It concerns the question of being, the meaning of being, which cannot be addressed as a purely formal question, since being is also a matter of *Fülle*, of fullness, content or fact. Stein's distinction between essential and real being (essences and essentialities having essential being, things, persons, animals and plants having real being) allows us to say that ontology deals exclusively with essential being, whereas metaphysics concerns all being, and in particular the meaning of being as such.

MOTIVATION

Motivation is the performing of one act because of another.

NATURE

The sphere determined by the lawfulness of causality.

ONTIC ANALYSIS

Ontic analysis is, in contrast with eidetic analysis the object of which is *a priori*, investigating something as existing in its concrete and factual complexity in the world. Stein's investigation concerning the state is an ontic analysis, not only addressing the essence of the state, but also the factual social complexity that renders the emergence of the state possible as a socially constructed sovereign subject of reference.

PHENOMENOLOGY

Stein's *Introduction to Philosophy* reveals that she understands phenomenology to occupy the centre of philosophy as such, so that this introduction in fact is an introduction to phenomenology. Her commitment to the description and discussion of experience as it is experienced is for her the ultimate philosophical commitment, which means that the kind of arguments she would accept against her philosophy are arguments drawn from experience as such. Phenomenology relies on the reduction of experience to its irreducible and indubitable structure: experience as experienced.

Conscious experience is structured by intentionality, i.e. by there being something experienced and an I experiencing in every conscious (i.e. constituted) experience.

PSYCHE

The psyche is constituted from those acts in which life power manifests itself.

SCIENCE

A science is identified by its object, i.e. by that of which it is the science. It involves all investigations which relate meaningfully to this object. The primary task of phenomenology is to clarify the objects of the various sciences, in order to facilitate the work and collaboration of the scientists.

SPIRIT

Motivatedness.

THE GIVEN

Given is everything that can be investigated phenomenologically. Phenomena, things, objects, essences, experiences and *a priori* relationships are all given.

THE THINGS THEMSELVES

Zur Sachen selbst! was the phenomenological slogan. Its purpose was to remind phenomenologists not to stay attached to thought systems or dogmas of any kind, but to proceed to clarity from engagement with the experience of things themselves.

VALUE AND VALUATION

A value is an objective motivating power, which is allowed to motivate concretely when accepted as mine by means of valuation.

Chronology of Stein's Works

To favour an overview, most minor works or translations of no direct relevance for this introduction have not been included. The publication year has been given if the work was published during Stein's life time. Otherwise the approximate final year of its composition is given. For a complete chronology see: Marianne Sawicki and IASPES: <http://edithsteincircle.com/biography/chronology-of-writings.html>. Some dates remain the object of scholarly debate.

Abbreviations

Aufbau	*Aufbau der menschlichen Person* (ESGA 14)
Beiträge	*Beiträge zur philosopischen Begründung der Psychologie und der Geisteswissenschaften* (ESGA 6)
Bildung	*Bildung und Entfaltung der Individualität* (ESGA 16)
CWES	*Collected Works of Edith Stein* (Washington DC: ICS Publications)
DV	Translation-commentary of Aquinas' *De veritate* (ESGA 23–4)
EES	*Endliches und ewiges Sein* (ESGA 11–12)
Einfühlung	*Zum Problem der Einfühlung* (ESGA 5)
Einführung	*Einführung in der Philosophie* (ESGA 8)
ESGA	*Edith Stein Gesamtwerke* (Freiburg – Basel – Vienna: Herder, 2000–14)
ESW	*Edith Steins Werke* (Freiburg – Basel – Vienna: Herder, 1977–99)
FEB	*Finite and Eternal Being* (ESGA 11–12/CWES IX)
Frau	*Die Frau* (ESGA 13)
HA	'Martin Heidegger's Existential Philosophy', transl. M. Lebech, Appendix to EES
Ideas	Edmund Husserl: *Ideas pertaining to a pure Phenomenology and to a phenomenological Philosophy*
Life	*Life in a Jewish Family* (ESGA 1/CWES 1, transl. J. Koeppel)
Mensch	*Was ist der Mensch?* (ESGA 15)
PPH	*Philosophy of Psychology and the Humanities* (ESGA 6/CWES 7, transl. M.C. Baseheart and M. Sawicki)
PA	*Potency and Act* (ESGA 10/CWES 11, transl. W. Redmond)
PE	*On the Problem of Empathy* (ESGA 5/CWES 3, transl. W. Stein)

State   *An Investigation Concerning the State* (ESGA 7/CWES
          10, transl. M. Sawicki)
SC   *Science of the Cross* (ESGA 18/CWES 6, transl. J. Koeppel)
Woman   *Woman* (CWES 2, transl. F. Oben)

Introduction

Stein's work is notoriously difficult to access. This is paradoxically not because her writings are difficult to read, they are written in plain and handsome German, and with a stringency seldom matched. It is the very stringency however, together with the fact that Stein rarely repeats herself, which accounts for the fact that it takes a long time to get through a few pages. To get the full picture moreover, one must not only expect to have one's categories rearranged, one will also have to start at the beginning, since Stein never repeats herself. As Stein's works amount to twenty-seven volumes, many give up, or content themselves with knowing that there is something there one might read one day.

This collection of essays provides a series of shortcuts. It brings together previously published articles revised for the purpose of providing both an overall picture of Stein's work as well as twelve self-contained introductions to specific aspects of it. If read from beginning to end some repetitions occur. It is hoped these can be of benefit to the beginner, and be to the specialist an occasion for assessing my interpretation.

The collection is divided into two parts reflecting the development of Stein's thought. The first one is entitled 'Phenomenology' and deals with the features of Stein's phenomenology which sets it apart from that of other phenomenologists', notably Husserl's. The second part is called 'Metaphysics' and treats of those of Stein's works that testify to her gradual understanding of the importance of the Christian faith for the completion of the phenomenological project and for acceding to a view of the existing world in its entirety.

The main concern of Stein's work is how to reconcile phenomenological and metaphysical thought. All of the chapters in this book contribute to clarify how she sees and accomplishes this task. Three of the chapters make use of Stein's thought to investigate subjects Stein did not herself explicitly attend to: Chapter 5 thus investigates human dignity, Chapter 6 the Christianity of Europe and Chapter 12 dementia, by deploying Stein's thought to approach these topics. The remainder of the chapters (except the first) are arranged so as to reflect Stein's development, many of them treating of several of Stein's works from both the early and later periods.

Chapter 1 provides an overview of Stein's work and situates it as that of a European philosopher. Although of Jewish descent, Stein understood herself as belonging on the continent of Europe. Moreover, Stein's philosophy is rooted in European philosophy, and it is to European philosophy that she understood herself to contribute.

Part I includes 5 chapters relating to Stein's early phenomenological thought, as it manifests itself in *On the Problem of Empathy*, *Philosophy of Psychology and the Humanities*, *Introduction to Philosophy* and *An Investigation concerning the State*.

Chapter 2 introduces Stein's phenomenology of the body as presented in *On the Problem of Empathy*, while situating it in the context of inter-subjective constitution as outlined in *Philosophy of Psychology and the Humanities*. It is argued that Stein's descriptive phenomenology, conjugated as it is by her understanding of inter-subjective constitution, makes her stand out among phenomenologists and makes her perspective particularly relevant to contemporary thought.

Chapter 3 gives a sketch of Stein's phenomenological value theory. Values are explored in their essential relatedness to motivation and to objective and subjective spirit on the one hand and in their role for the formation of the personality and character of the person on the other. The chapter looks at how values are experienced, at what that tells us about their objectivity, and at what the experience of values allows us to know about ourselves.

Chapter 4 explains how it is the community-forming ability of values that make them of decisive importance for the state, since the state is a community or at least relies on community. To explain what this means the relationship between personality and the various types of constituting a 'we' (mass, association and community) is explored and discussed in their relation to the state. Finally, the question concerning the specific type of value response upon which the state relies is addressed to achieve a sketch of the social construction of the state.

Chapter 5 explains that because Stein's phenomenology includes an understanding of the motivatedness of the constitution of objects, an analysis of value and motivation, and an epistemological (interpretative) notion of 'type', it becomes possible to show how and why we identify human dignity as the fundamental value of the human being. Although Stein does not develop the notion of human dignity herself in any great detail, her phenomenology, because of the above-mentioned special features, enables us to conduct a constitutional analysis, not only of the human being who is the subject of this value, but also of the value we reasonably must place on it, given this value's foundational relationships with other values. The chapter explores Stein's phenomenological description of value and valuation, proceeds to a constitutional analysis of the human being to whom fundamental value might be attributed, and finally shows how it comes about that we identify this being, the human being, as being of fundamental value.

Chapter 6 deploys Stein's education theory, community theory and value theory to clarify Christianity's identity generating power in Europe. As a child grows up it contributes to the community first and foremost by the affirmation of its own identity. This makes the process of education of equal importance to the individual and to the community. Jesus' affirmation of his identity made his followers give him the titles of Prophet, Eternal High Priest and King of Kings, thus giving him a status like one of the elders in charge of opening up the possibilities for the young. It is as such that he marks inter-subjective space, particularly in Europe, where kings made use of his authority to rule in his name.

Part II includes six chapters dealing with issues relating to Stein's later thought as expressed in her essays on education, woman, phenomenology and ontology, *The Structure of the Human Being*, *What is the Human Being?*, the translation-commentary of Aquinas' *De veritate*, *Potency and Act*, *Finite and Eternal Being* and *Science of the Cross*.

Chapter 7 argues that it is because the image we have of the human person determines educational practice that Stein's philosophy of education consists in anthropology. Her main work in education theory falls into two parts, philosophical and theological, as both disciplines influence our image of the human person. *The Structure of the Human Person*, the first and philosophical part of this foundational project, constitutes Stein's mature philosophy of the human person – a subject that had occupied her all her life. This chapter examines the philosophical anthropology of this work, its historical background and its place within Stein's entire work.

Chapter 8 discusses Stein's philosophy of woman. It circumscribes the place of the philosophy of woman and of gender within the whole of Stein's philosophy, in particular her philosophical anthropology. Some typical differences of the sexes as perceived by Stein are outlined and discussed.

Chapter 9 looks at Stein's Thomism. After her baptism in 1922 Stein engaged with Aquinas on several levels. Initially she compared Aquinas' thought with that of Husserl, then proceeded to translate several of his works, and attempted to explore some of his fundamental concepts ('potency' and 'act') phenomenologically. She arrived finally in *Finite and Eternal Being* at a philosophical position inspired by his synthesis of Christian faith and philosophical tradition without abandoning her phenomenological starting point and method. It is argued that whether one would want to call this position 'Thomist' depends on what one understands Thomism to be.

Chapter 10 is a beginner's guide to reading *Finite and Eternal Being*, which Stein called her 'spiritual legacy'. So far the access to that legacy has been restricted by the difficulty of identifying exactly what it is that Stein is doing in the work. What is clear, however, is that Stein understood her task as being that of bringing together Medieval and Modern philosophy, the latter represented by phenomenology and the former by St Thomas in particular. We can thus see the work as the culmination of Stein's phenomenological project, as well as a work standing in the tradition of the *philosophia perennis*.

Chapter 11 pursues the interpretation of *Finite and Eternal Being* by the means of analysing one of the appendices to *Finite and Eternal Being*, entitled 'Martin Heidegger's Existentialist Philosophy'. It asks why Stein wrote about Heidegger before turning to her discussion of Heidegger's project. Finally Stein's and Heidegger's alternative phenomenological inheritance and their relationship are outlined.

Chapter 12 discusses dementia in the light of Stein's work, in particular her final work *Science of the Cross*. The biggest challenge presented to us by dementia is that we are in need of a reflection on who we are ourselves, so as to enable recognition of the one affected by dementia. To enable this, the structure of the human person proposed by Stein is reiterated, and the act of empathy, in which we are aware of the experience of the other, is deployed to access the experience of the one who is suffering from dementia. Finally, the one suffering from dementia is compared with the person living through the mystical experience of the 'dark night of the soul', as the latter is described by St John of the Cross, and discussed in Stein's final work *The Science of the Cross*.

***

References to Stein's work are given by title of work, chapter and section number wherever possible in order to facilitate the use of different editions and translations. Whenever page numbers are also given in a reference they refer mostly to the English translation, except when otherwise indicated in the text. Quotations have been taken from the English translations of Stein's works by ICS Publications when these exist, unless otherwise indicated. All translations taken from works not yet published in the *Collected Works of Edith Stein* are my own.

Edith Stein as a European Philosopher

The Silesian philosopher Edith Stein is best known for her philosophy of the person. Her engagement with the relationship between personal and social identity is often overlooked however, along with her refined phenomenology of the social world resulting from this engagement. We shall in this first chapter look at how this engagement is rooted in her own experience of controversial social identity (as a German Jew in Silesia/Schlesien/Śląsk), and how it in turn forces us to understand her, beyond ethnic boundaries, as a European (1). We shall then look at the European roots of Stein's philosophy, particularly in the traditions stemming from Husserl and Aquinas (2). Finally we shall attempt to show how her Christian philosophy is founded on her phenomenological engagement with social identity and may be seen as an attempt to solve the problems arising from various forms of colliding nationalism (3).

Stein as a European

Growing up in Silesia marked Stein's thought significantly. Although she saw herself as a Prussian, the changeable history of Silesia was nevertheless her background. After the First World War some members of her family moved to Berlin from Polish speaking areas in Silesia as these ceased to be German territory. Silesia was also earlier under Austrian (1526–1742) and Bohemian (1335–1526) rule, and in the early Middle Ages it was first Moravian and then Polish. It is the latter, for most of its extent, again today.[1] The shifting territorial boundaries drifting over the landscape like clouds made Stein realise, much earlier than most young people, that the state is a reality that is not essentially linked to a specific landscape or to a specific people. Her being Jewish contributed, probably significantly, to this realisation which she was able to write down after the observation of the impact of the First World War on the landscape of her *Heimat* in her *An Investigation concerning the State* (1925). This work was written mostly in Wrocław/Breslau in the years just after the end of the First World War and reflects the complicated conditions of her home country in such a manner as to facilitate the determination of the essence of the state. The possibilities of eidetic variation brought out by the seismic political changes during and after the war allowed her to understand the state *as* sovereignty. That the state is sovereign means that it can determine and uphold positive law in principle and in reality. When it cannot do that (as when it is taken over by another state or divided), it ceases to exist. The people, which perhaps constituted the community that allowed the state to come into existence in the first place, does not by this fact cease to exist; it has its own principle of constitution, determined among other things by a common culture, history and language.[2] The state can both foster and hinder the development of this cultural community with the power expressing itself in its sovereignty. Towards the inside, the state subjects and organises its citizens under its law by means of its power in order to consolidate itself. Towards the outside, the state affirms its sovereignty among the other states and defends its territory. In so far as the defining characteristic of the state is its sovereignty, the state is neither of positive nor negative value. It is sometimes good, as when it organises the human community in such a way that it can flourish and express itself through its art and culture. But it is sometimes bad, as when it sacrifices human life, destroys families and thwarts the creative unfolding of cultural life, in

1   Helmut Neubach, *Kleine Geschichte Schlesiens* (Görlitz: Senfkorn, 2007).
2   Habermas makes a like distinction between nation and state in 'The European Nation-State: On the Past and Future of Sovereignty and Citizenship' in *The Inclusion of the Other*, ed. by Ciaran Cronin and Pablo DeGreif (Cambridge: Polity Press, 2002), Chapter 4.

order to protect its sovereignty. It was possibly Stein's understanding of the value-neutrality of the state that made her chose not to engage with politics as a career path, something she may have toyed with as a young woman before the First World War.³ It may also have been this insight that made her ask for baptism, in so far as it forced her to realise that there had to be a community that would engage persons at a deeper level than the state did, if persons were, as she thought they were, to unfold in community. At any rate *An Investigation concerning the State* is the last work written by Stein before her conversion.

Understanding that the state provides no final destiny, Stein is Silesian *and* Prussian, German *and* Polish, Jewish *and* Christian.⁴ She can be all these because she identified herself first and foremost as a human being, subordinating all other types of collective identity to this one.⁵ But she realised that a state, trying to consolidate itself as a *nation* state, *could* disregard all collective identities other than the ones it took to form the basis of its social integration, and as a consequence be a grave danger to those individuals whose identity it was not prepared to accommodate. Stein is a European philosopher by default, since Europe is the smallest location that fits her national identification comfortably.⁶

3 Alasdair McIntyre, *Edith Stein: A Philosophical Prologue* (Oxford: Continuum – Rowman and Littlefield, 2006), chapter 11.

4 Stein did not identify herself as Polish, and she did not speak Polish fluently. Today, however, to say where she came from, we might find it easier to say she came from Poland. The point made here is that that would not be wrong.

5 We shall investigate the possibility of preferring the human type above all others in Chapter 6.

6 In Chapter 5 we shall argue that Europe is also specifically marked by Christianity, and as Stein in her mature years identified herself very much as a Christian, this feature of European cultural life would have had importance for her.

Husserl and Aquinas

To live as a human being in a place, in a landscape and in a culture means
to live with these in a constant exchange. It means to take root in these and
to be marked by these. It also means to contribute to this place, this landscape, this culture. Stein became a European philosopher in precisely this
sense: she stands in the European philosophical tradition, in the stream of
European cultural life. She is penetrated by both of these and contributes
something to both. This did not happen by accident: her precise descriptions of the spiritual participation in a community shows clearly that she
regarded the reception, interpretation and creation of cultural objects,
reading and writing, as participation in this cultural community.[7] A spiritual community sources its energy and nourishes itself from such participation. Stein's 'method' for such participation is the 'method' of life:
it is thinking about, thinking through, thinking on, learning from those
who went before about the matters they thought about – not staying *at*
their thought, but looking through it to the *things themselves*, and judging it in the light of these things. The influence of Dilthey on Stein's phenomenology makes her specific kind of phenomenology seem particularly
hermeneutical.[8] Whenever Stein is doing phenomenology, she is in fact
also doing hermeneutics, being aware, as she is, that all objects motivate
by their value and are constituted fully (i.e. identified and understood)
only when they are also constituted in their value.[9] Constituting things in
their value involves the person in its entirety, in the hermeneutic process
which constitutes the spiritual breathing of the cultural community and
of the individual person alike. Precisely this hermeneutic feature allows
her to enter into thought structures that otherwise are of a different kind

7   E.g. PPH, II, §2, e).
8   See Anna Jani, 'Von der Welterfahrung zur geistigen Welt. Spuren der Dilthey-
     Rezeption in Edith Steins frühen Schriften' forthcoming in the *Edith Stein Jahrbuch*
     2015.
9   State, II, Introduction, p. 147.

compared to phenomenology. It allows her to follow thinking that has a different point of departure, to think it through and continue it according to its own principles. This process of following through is the process we assist at when we read her interpretations of texts written by others. It accounts for some of the difficulties associated with reading Stein, since she thinks through to that which the texts concern, in order to learn from it how to assess them. When this is done, one understands not only the text, but also that which the text concerns, as well as one's own standpoint in relation to the text. The interpretation can have greater or lesser depth: some things remain hidden from the superficial awareness, which may be seen by the one who has a deeper understanding. Living in and learning from the cultural world in a constant exchange is the normal environment in which we develop by deepening as persons.

It is well known that Stein's philosophy is particularly rooted in the thought of two other Europeans: in the thought of the twentieth-century philosopher Edmund Husserl on the one hand, and in that of the thirteenth-century philosopher-theologian Thomas Aquinas on the other hand. Behind these two stand many other European thinkers: behind Husserl in particular Descartes, Berkeley, Hume, Kant and Brentano and behind Aquinas in particular Aristotle, Plato, Pseudo-Dionysius and Augustine.[10] Besides this broad spectrum of philosophical forbears, other European thinkers, including the Spanish mystics Theresa of Avila and John of the Cross, influenced Stein: Hegel, Darwin, Dilthey, Scheler, Pfänder, Reinach, Conrad-Martius, Ingarden, Heidegger and Lipps, to mention but some. We shall here concentrate on the main influences on Stein's philosophy: Husserl and Aquinas.

In Husserl it was the phenomenological project that so fascinated Stein that she moved from Breslau to Göttingen to participate in it and contribute to it.[11] The phenomenological project to found the sciences

10 Pseudo-Dionysius was perhaps Syrian, perhaps Byzantine, and Augustine was Carthage in North Africa. Further afield Aquinas was also influenced by also the Spanish-Moroccan Averroes and the Persian Avicenna.
11 See Life, Chapters 5 and 7.

is one of the oldest European intellectual projects, taken up by Husserl in a new manner to overcome the tensions after the Reformation and to reconcile the modern epistemological concerns with the classical project. For Stein this new manner was convincing, because it offered a point of departure in something that could not be doubted: *experience as such*. This point of departure in experience as such is the phenomenological starting point, which Husserl attempted to clarify from Descartes' insight, that in the experience of doubt the certainty of the experience of doubting is indubitably hidden. With this experience of the experience that cannot be doubted the entire field of phenomenological investigation is opened: all that is experienced can be investigated *as such* (i.e. as experienced), as the precise and meticulous description of it remains within the sphere of the indubitable.

Stein appropriated the phenomenological programme early in her life, with the effect that she later could not or would not think without it. From it she had an understanding of the modern project, which made this programme necessary; the response to the sceptical challenge posed and provided by Modernity was a response to a challenge Stein understood as her own, and indeed as philosophy's own. Stein could learn from Neo-Kantianism, Idealism and Hegelianism with Husserl, because she relied on the phenomenological starting point to test the epistemological foundations of the thought systems and concepts of these thinkers. Later she made aspects of Aquinas', Aristotle's and Neo-Platonist' thought her own, because she already had a methodological approach that allowed her to reflect on and assess their fundamental concepts from experience itself and bring them into concert with each other on a phenomenological basis.

Stein's departure from Husserlian phenomenology, if one can speak about departure, happened already from the outset, with the emphasis on empathy being the indispensable foundation for an inter-subjective understanding of objectivity. With her analysis of empathy Stein obtained the possibility to understand and analyse the structure of the social world. In her *Philosophy of Psychology and the Humanities* she consolidated her understanding of inter-subjective constitution. In and through these studies

she maintained Husserl's and Reinach's emphasis on the *a priori* intuitability of essences, so that she regarded objectivity to be given in three ways:
subjectively, *a priori* and inter-subjectively.

From Aquinas Stein learnt an approach that addresses being directly.
Yet Aquinas' reliance on Aristotle's metaphysics meant that his understanding of essence was not immediately reconcilable with the phenomenological one. This makes Stein undertake a critical examination
of Aristotle's metaphysics, the conclusion of which is that it pursues a
concept of essence that has two irreconcilable goals: on the one hand
it is meant to secure substance as fundamental in its concretion and on
the other it is supposed to designate the kind of the thing, such that
the essence of a thing is its kind. Instead Stein insists on the intelligibility of the essence in the individual and regards the essence of the kind,
type or species as founded upon this essence. The most important thing
Stein learned from Aquinas was that Revelation can and must contribute
something essential to philosophy, if philosophy wants to remain faithful to its fundamental pursuit of giving an account of the whole of the
existing world.

Christianity above and beyond inter-subjectivity

Stein regarded the state as not only transient but also as value-neutral.
Her understanding of community, in contrast, is that persons are not only
capable of community, but that they are by their spiritual being essentially
immersed in it and open to it. In her final works Stein comes to see this as
a reflection of God's Trinitarian nature in the human being. In the middle
period, her reflection on the theme of community takes the form of reflection on education and education theory. Her main work in this area is her
double work on educational anthropology, *The Structure of the Human
Person – What is the Human Being?*, conceived as the foundation for a
Catholic education theory, and thought out against the background of the

incubation of the Third Reich.[12] The Nazi ideology relied on national identity to implement its claim for sovereignty. As Stein saw national identity as
one of the possibilities the human being has to form part of a community
which does not necessarily allow for a peaceful realisation, her educational
anthropology is in fact a statement of the centrality and indispensability
of the idea of the human person to education. To finally answer, however,
the question of the beginning and end of the human being, Stein affirms
that recourse to Revelation cannot be dispensed with, as no answer can
be given to these questions by philosophy alone. This is how her Christian
philosophy is inaugurated: by the idea that we cannot know who we are
apart from God and the revelation of his love in Jesus Christ. In this way
Stein's philosophy of the person and of community finds a foundation in a
Christian philosophy having the Trinity as its centre, a Christian philosophy that comes to be as a result of the awareness of the transitoriness of the
state and of the accidental fatalities related to national identity.

***

That national communities consolidating in states can become lethal to
human beings who do not belong to them, may be a hard lesson we are still
learning in the process of globalisation. The solution Stein is proposing is
one that can be accomplished only from within by the individual him or
herself. It involves awareness of one's own identity and of being in charge
of it through one's process of identification facilitated by education. It also
involves 'walking at the hand of the Lord', in that it is only in the Kingdom
of God that the human being will find its ultimate identity as a member
of the community that is the whole Christ.

12   We shall treat of Stein's education theory in Chapter 7, and of her related philosophy
      of woman in Chapter 8. Chapter 6 on the formation of the Christianity of Europe
      also deal with the education of the European.

PART I

Phenomenology

CHAPTER 2

The Constitution of the Body

In *On the Problem of Empathy* Stein presents a phenomenology of the body which forms part of a constitutional analysis of the psycho-physical individual. To approach it, we shall start by situating her work in relation to that of Husserl and other phenomenologists of the time (1). Then we shall characterise the nature of inter-subjective constitution according to her later *Philosophy of Psychology and the Humanities*, since the body is also inter-subjectively constituted (2). Finally we turn to the analysis of the body as it is found in her doctoral dissertation (3).

Stein's place in the phenomenological movement

Stein became Husserl's assistant following the death of Adolph Reinach during the First World War. In that capacity she was editor of *Ideas* II and III. But before that she had already attempted to underpin Husserl's understanding that empathy was foundational for inter-subjectivity by writing her doctoral dissertation on the topic. *On the Problem of Empathy* (1917) originally comprised a hermeneutic analysis (now lost) of various occurrences of the theme in authors influencing the early stirrings of phenomenology such as Theodor Lipps, Max Scheler and Wilhelm Dilthey. This led up to an eidetic analysis of the essence of empathy (which is now the first chapter) and two constitutional analyses pertaining to what empathy contributes to the constitution of: the psycho-physical individual (Chapter Three) and the person (Chapter Four). In these analyses Stein follows what she understands to be the standard phenomenological practice, and models her work on what she already knows of the overall project of Husserl's *Ideas*. She thus begins with a historical/empirical analysis of how the concept has been formed by others before her (the chapter now lost), proceeds to an analysis of essential structures (in the same way as *Ideas* I does), moves on to constitutional issues (like those treated in *Ideas* II), before turning towards the sciences consequent upon the things thus constituted (as does *Ideas* III).

Because it allows us to access inter-subjective experience, empathy is at the heart of the phenomenological project. *On the Problem of Empathy* is therefore a kind of addition to *Ideas* I; something Stein understood to be missing in this work for the work to be complete. Later, when her attempt to edit *Ideas* II and III for publication had left her convinced that Husserl did not understand the importance of this addition, she wrote her own contribution to the phenomenological project of founding the sciences. She focused on psychology and the humanities the objects of which (psyche and spirit) she knew to be most affected in their constitution by the lack of an appropriate analysis of empathy.[1] Already the analyses of the constitution of psyche and spirit in *On the Problem of Empathy* are superior in their systematic precision to the analyses of *Ideas* II. But the two lines of enquiry are still further pursued in the two treatises post-dating her editorial work, with *Sentient Causality* exploring the constitution of the psyche and *Individual and Community* the foundation of the humanities. These two treatises make up what is known today as *Philosophy of Psychology and the Humanities*. It may be possible to understand Husserl's declining to publish *Ideas* II and III as an acknowledgement of the fact that Stein with this work had accomplished something that superseded these.

Apart from Husserl, Scheler, Lipps and Dilthey, two other important influences on her early work must be mentioned: Alexander Pfänder and Adolph Reinach. Both were members of the Munich circle, and both had an interest in practical philosophy, i.e. in matters relating to the will and

---

1   Marianne Sawicki: 'Making up Husserl's Mind about Constitution', in *Yearbook of the Irish Philosophical Society* 2007, ed. Will Desmond, pp. 191–216, and *Body Text and Science* (Dordrecht: Kluwer, 2000). Husserl worked his way round to give the *Cartesian Meditations* in 1929, which affords to empathy a less important role for knowledge, sufficiently founded in the transcendental ego.

normativity. From Reinach she took a rudimentary theory of values as well as insight into objective (*a priori*) normative relations. From Pfänder she took a phenomenology of the will, which she combined with Scheler's theory of community to form an understanding of the formation of character and a theory of the relationship between valuation, character and community.

The nature of inter-subjective constitution

For Stein, as well as for Husserl and all the early phenomenologists, constitutional analysis is part and parcel of the phenomenological method: it is an analysis of how something is brought together or comes together, how it is identified in experience from various elements or sources.[2] A cup is constituted from various acts of seeing, touching, remembering, using, comparing etc.; it comes together against the background of other experiences (e.g. green, textured, heavy, moody, etc.) which recede to the background or become qualities of the cup when the cup is constituted as such. Furthermore, the cup is constituted as objective in the field of tension between subjective experience and inter-subjective experience accessed by the means of empathy: You see a cup – I think 'there probably is a cup' – you point it out – I see a cup. My experience and your experience comes to me as something that can be challenged by the experience of others (including myself), so that *your* experience, and even *our* experience does not necessarily coincide with *mine*.

The different types of interdependence of subjective experience that structures inter-subjectivity are discussed by Stein in her treatise *Individual and Community*. Here she shows how *sentient contagion* (involving psychic transference of conviction without awareness of the objective motivating

---

2   This includes non-'thingly' matters like time and space, which are also constituted from various elements or aspects of experiences.

power of values); *association* (relying on acts of will where subjects relate to one another according to objective characteristics) and *community* (constituted from shared value response resulting in a common life) allow for different types of collective experience, which I may identify as 'our' experience depending on how I identify myself in relation to them. The constitution of my personal self (as part of this community, member of that association, influenced by this group) thus defines not only how I experience the world, but also the type of inter-subjective experience I will contribute to the constitution (the social construction) of the world for others.

The understanding of how constitution, and hence experience, is motivated is the proper object of the sciences of the humanities,[3] and Stein therefore envisages motivated constitution as something that can be explored in them, e.g. in anthropology, sociology, politics, history, literature and art. Also the natural sciences can be studied by the humanities. It is, for example, possible to make an anthropological study of how experimental chemistry is conducted in a particular medical laboratory in Texas, and it is also possible to write the history of astronomy. The body and its constitution as influenced by culture are often examined by the various sciences of the humanities. What they investigate is the motivation behind particular types of constitution. Because the body incarnates subjects which in turn are co-constitutors of the world, and hence manifests, like no other object, a source of objectivity, it tends to be controversial. That the body can also be investigated by the various branches of medicine with its support disciplines of biochemistry, physics and mathematical statistics in no way precludes, but in fact presupposes, that the body is inter-subjectively constituted in the first place. If, for example, we consider abortion to be an acceptable medical practice, we can do so for various reasons:

1.   We can consider it acceptable because we see the practice as a healthy social practice not harming anyone or any*body*. We then do it because we value the advantages associated with abortion (e.g. family planning,

---

3   *Geisteswissenschaften* is the German for humanities. In German: 'Geist' means 'spirit', and Stein understands spirit as motivatedness.

population control) higher than the lives of the foetuses being aborted. In this case we do not recognise the foetuses as experiencing persons having bodies like other persons.

2. We can also consider abortion acceptable because the Medical Association of which we are members decides to accept the practice and to support its legality. We then do it because we have decided to be a member of this association (and because we value this membership higher than our own opinion).

3. Finally, we can do it 'because everyone thinks it is a good idea', i.e. by following whatever is believed to be right at this particular time. We then do it because we have been infected with the value-response of others, and let ourselves be guided by the energy issuing from their motivation. When I do this, I am typically not aware of being contaminated with conviction, although others might well be aware of the sentient contagion.

'Our' attitude to anything at all is composed from these sources, and thus inter-subjectivity, i.e. the medium through which something is identified to be what it is ('an acceptable social practice', 'a cup', 'a human being'), is composed accordingly.

It remains, of course, that the I's perspective is its own, i.e. that it is capable of comparing its own perspective on, or constitution of, something with that of the 'we' it co-constitutes and takes as decisive for its inter-subjective constitution. It also remains capable of comparing alternative 'we's', i.e., comparing the constitution of the world that they give rise to. This means that I am faced with a choice – which the later existentialists will call existential – a choice of what motivates my constitution of the world, together with the 'we' I take as co-constituting it.

Having thus seen what empathy gives rise to: i.e. the inter-subjective constitution of the world and the constitution of inter-subjectivity, let us now return to the treatise on empathy to see how the body is constituted according to it.

The constitutional analysis of the body in
On the Problem of Empathy

On the Problem of Empathy does not primarily analyse how the act of empathy is constituted (although Chapter II on the essence of empathy implicitly does that). Rather it analyses how *those entities that could not be constituted without the contribution of the act of empathy* (because they are subjective in nature) are constituted: i.e. the psycho-physical individual (including its parts: body, soul, psyche, emotions, character) and the person (in its spiritual space defined by motivation and concretised by a personality relative to chosen values). Stein is in other words analysing how the body, the soul, the psyche and the spirit 'comes together' for us, how it happens that we experience ourselves as we do. We cannot really say that this presupposes that we in fact have body, soul and spirit – Stein is rather showing what the experiences are that contribute to us identifying ourselves as having these. Constitution cannot be forced: identification is essentially motivated. Our understanding of our body is motivated by our experience in its entirety.

So what is this experience that allows us to identify ourselves and our bodies?

'I', the pure I, constitutes itself from experience as the quality-less pole or subject of all experience. Thus the I is always there, essentially related to experience. However, that is the only thing which is essentially related to experience. The other and the body are not quite essentially related to experience, only to the type of experience which is recognisably ours:

> In various authors, such as Lipps, we have found the interpretation that this [I] is not an 'individual "I"' but first becomes individual in contrast with 'you' and 'he'. What does this individuality mean? First of all, it means only that it is 'itself' and no other. This 'selfness' is experienced and is the basis of all that is 'mine'. Naturally it is first brought into relief in contrast with another when another is given. This other is at first not qualitatively distinguished from it, since both are quality-less, but only distinguished simply as an 'other'. This otherness is apparent in the type of givenness; it is other than 'I' because it is given to me in another way than 'I'. Therefore it is 'you'. But since it experiences itself as I experience myself, the 'you'

is another 'I'. Thus the 'I' does not become individualised because another faces it, but its individuality, or as we should rather say (because we must reserve the term 'individuality' for something else), its selfness is brought into relief in contrast with the otherness of the other.[4]

Stein does not think that the body is the principle of individuation of the I (as does for example Aquinas, whom she later criticises for this),[5] nor that it is 'before' constitution as Marianne Sawicki claims it is in her otherwise brilliant analysis of Stein's editorial work on *Ideas* II.[6] The latter idea would have compromised Stein's adherence to the phenomenological method. The body is constituted, for Stein, because it is the best way of making sense of what we in fact experience, but this is a matter of fact, not of necessity.

When this is said, I do experience my I as experiencing a stream of experiences that seems organised according to patterns such that fields of experience can be distinguished according to what I must identify as different senses: the fields of vision, hearing, touch etc. These patterns, Stein affirms, are the material from which the soul is constituted as the substantive root of that specific set of abilities, including the ability to place things into categories, which is mine. Not only do I experience my experience as peculiarly structured, I also experience my I as embodied. The body is persistently there when I experience myself, and that in different ways. It is given in outer perception to be sure, but not in that alone. If it were, we would have

> the strangest object. This would be a real thing, a physical body, whose motivated successive appearances exhibit striking gaps. It would withhold its rear side with more stubbornness than the moon.[7]

Besides exhibiting these gaps, some of which I might be able to reach by touch (the back of my head), but not see, it also has the peculiarity that I cannot walk away from it:

---

4   PE, III, 1.
5   See Chapter 9.
6   *Body, Text and Science*, Chapter 2.
7   PE, III, 4, a; p. 41.

I can approach and withdraw from any other thing, can turn toward or away from it. [... It is ...] given to me in an infinitely variable multiplicity of appearances and of changing positions, and there are also times when it is not given to me. But this one object (my physical body) is given to me in successive appearances only variable within very narrow limits. As long as I have my eyes open at all, it is continually there with a steadfast obtrusiveness, always having the same tangible nearness as no other object has. It is always 'here' while other objects are always 'there.'[8]

Moreover, I sense my body in all its parts, so that this 'here' where I am (my zero point of orientation), is extended in space: the sensations arising from all the entities making up my body are amalgamated into a unity, so that the unity of my living body is constituted as taking up space from the sensations of all these places. The unity of the sensed body is constituted as the same as the outwardly perceived body:

I not only see my hand and bodily perceive it as sensing, but I also 'see' its fields of sensation constituted for me in bodily perception. [...] This is exactly analogous to the province of outer perception. We not only see the table and feel its hardness, we also 'see' its hardness. [...] The seen living body does not remind us it can be the scene of manifold sensations. Neither is it merely a physical thing taking up the same space as the living body given as sensitive in bodily perception. It is given as a sensing, living body.[9]

Movement, sensations (*Empfindungen*) like pain and pleasure, moods and spiritual feelings (*Gefühle*) are all experienced in the body; they are constituted from bodily experience. The body is thus, as a whole, a sophisticated sense organ that allows me to interact as a constituting I with a material world that makes sense. I find myself experiencing in my body and by means of it.

But if I had only my own experience to sample it is quite possible I would never get to constitute this world as meaningful or as separate from my body. I would not identify what is experienced in the body as something dependent on *my* bodily nature rather than on the world as it is. Without empathy, I would think that the world is as I feel it is. But in

8   PE, III, 4 (b), pp. 41–2.
9   Ibid., pp. 44–5.

fact (again not by necessity) I have the experience of the other to sample from by means of empathy. Just as I 'see' my own fields of sensation (the sensitivity of the hand), I see those of the other, whose body I have learnt to constitute according to the same type as my own:

> The hand resting on the table does not lie there like the book beside it. It 'presses' against the table more or less strongly; it lies there limpid or stretched; and I 'see' these sensations of pressure and tension in a con-primordial way.[10]

Sensory empathy, which I also have with animals and to a limited extent with plants, is the type of empathy that allows me to 'feel into' what the other is feeling (sluggish, content, threatened) although this feeling is motivated by a value only a spiritual 'I' can identify as such (the good, the pleasant, the threatening as such). I would only know this, however, when I have learnt to do it and therefore am capable of spiritual empathy. This, in contrast with sensory empathy, is what enables me to identify and understand spiritual persons, i.e. I's who consciously perform one mental act because of another. It involves understanding the other's motivations (why he thinks he does what he does, as distinct from why he does what he does – I can also know the latter of animals and plants), and these motivations can be followed in so far as what is felt gets expressed in a glance, an attitude, in language or in art.

I do not necessarily constitute myself as a spiritual person, i.e. I do not necessarily know that I am motivated. Were I to be raised among wolves, it seems that I would constitute myself on the type of the wolf, and consequently not learn language and categorisation, although I might well be capable of it for a while as a very young 'cub'. I might attempt to use my limbs as does the wolf, and not constitute the pain we would expect a child to feel using its hands and knees for running at speed as important. Education in a human community enables me to observe in others what I can find in myself, and it is indeed pointed out to me with great attention and care so that I would learn to identify myself as a person and consequently be able to take my place in society and be capable of what we call responsibility.

10 PE, III, 5 (a), p. 58.

Stein's constitutional analysis of the body thus shows how empathy, the act in which we relate to foreign experience, enables us to constitute our own body in parallel with that of the other on a type that can be varied (e.g. wolf, Martian, Irish, woman, human person).[11] The body is not fixed but allows for a continuum of interpretations characteristic of different communities. Stein's analysis in this way incorporates an aspect of social construction as it explores the significance of empathy for the constitution of the being that we are.

***

Stein's analysis of empathy allows for a diversified account of the constitution of inter-subjectivity, which in turn allows for a phenomenological clarification of the foundation of Psychology and the Humanities. Her analysis of the constitution of the body accounts for our experience of the way our experience is structured, seen from within as well as from the perspective of others. It explains why we experience the body as objective and subjective at the same time. In so far as we consider her contributions as contributions to the common phenomenological project, this project is given an analysis of the body that does not compromise the transcendental point of departure and an analysis of inter-subjective experience that relies on this uncompromised position.

11   See also Chapter 8.

CHAPTER 3

Motivation and Value

Stein's phenomenology of value and motivation integrates insights she found in Reinach, Scheler and Husserl. Where Reinach stressed the *a priori* of the values and Scheler the hierarchy they form, Husserl was interested in describing the act of valuation and sees values as founded on things.[1] Stein's account stands between Sartre's later subjectivist existentialism and Levinas' insistence on the Other as the ground of obligation.[2] Because of

1   Adolph Reinach, 'Die Überlegung: ihre etische und rechtliche Bedeutung', *Gesammelte Schriften*, pp. 121–6 and *Sämtliche Werke* pp. 279–311. See also Beate Beckmann: *Phänomenologie des religiösen Erlebnisses. Religionsphilosophische Überlegungen im Anschluss an Adolph Reinach und Edith Stein* (Würzburg: Königshausen und Neumann, 2003), pp. 90–2 and 196–208. Max Scheler, *Formalism in Ethics and Non-Formal Ethics of Values*, transl. by Frings and Funk (Evanston: Northwestern University Press, 1973) and *Ressentiment*, transl. by William W. Holdheim (New York: Schocken, 1972). Edmund Husserl, *Ideas II*, transl. by Rojcevicz and Schuwer (Dordrecht: Kluwer, 1989), Section III and *Vorlesungen über Ethik und Wertlehre*, Husserliana Bd. XXVIII. See also John Drummond's Introduction to *Phenomenological Approaches to Moral Philosophy. A Handbook* (Dordrecht: Kluwer, 2002).

2   John Drummond op. cit. gives up situating Stein as either a realist axiologist (understanding values to exist independently of the evaluator) or an idealist subjectivist (which existentialists or value constructivists could be said to be) and for good reason. She, like the early and middle Husserl, understands the constitution of values to rely on the subject as much as on the object constituted (which as constituted, and as inter-subjectively constituted, must have essence). This intentional structure of all experience is the key to the inseparability of subjective perspective and objective analysability in early transcendental phenomenology: Stein would understand the label 'transcendental' to refer to exactly this necessity, which could be likened to a Möbius band whose inner and outer side is so connected that it is neither and both. See her discussion of realism and idealism in *Einführung*, I, c) 5 and 7 (pp. 69–72 and 75–9) and Hans Rainer Sepp's discussion of it: 'Edith Steins Position in die

her ability to synthesise the best from Scheler and Husserl, and because she started with the notion of empathy that allowed her to include the hermeneutical tradition from Dilthey, Stein elaborates a phenomenological theory of motivation in which value plays the role of motivation's object or formal explanation (analogous to how the perceived is the specific object of perception and its formal explanation). Motivation is like perception in that it is experienced as identified by its object. It is unlike perception in that it is essentially felt and in that it can be followed or infelt (empathised) in others, in texts, and in other things marked by spirit.[3] Motivatedness reveals to us the entire inner world of persons and is in fact, according to Stein, what we understand by spirit.

It is the simplicity of this understanding – spirit is motivatedness – that allows Stein to develop her comprehensive theory of what in German is called the 'sciences of the spirit', and which we in English call 'the humanities' (*Geisteswissenschaften*). As values are what allow us to conceptualise what type of motivatedness we have in front of us, they also explain why something is done. When this is their function, we call them motives. Motives, like values, can be shared, in the same way as what is perceived can be seen by others. But unlike perception, shared motivation involves an inner dimension that allows for motivation to be shared at different levels in accordance with the structure of the persons motivated, so that inter-subjective constitution is layered, paralleling the layers of the person.[4] Motivation is power or life, like the spirit is, and analysing the values

---

idealismus-realismus Debatte' in Beckmann and Gerl-Falkovitz (eds), *Edith Stein. Themen Bezüge Dokumente* (Würzburg: Königshausen und Neumann, 2003). See also Chapter 9.

3   Perception as well can be empathised, but not really without empathising its motivation, what it feels like. What we see when seeing someone watch, is that they watch something, aeroplanes, for example. We might wonder why they do that, but then we are already preoccupied with motivations, just as we are, when we wonder what they are watching. Motivations, generally speaking, interest us far more than the sheer perception of things, as this perception only makes sense in relation to its motivation.

4   The figure below shows the various ways in which the different layers of the person allow for different types of sociality. The value response of the person is further

in which this power is conceptualised as originating or as objective, must be accompanied by an analysis of valuation, which is the act in which I allow this power to flow into my life stream and direct it, the act in which I constitute the values as mine.

Let us first look at how values are experienced according to Stein (1). Then we will have to ask what that tells us about what they are, and what reasons we have to affirm that they are what we think they are (2). And finally we will have to ask what that allows us to know about ourselves (3).

The experience of values

Experience, to Stein, is what is left when the phenomenological and transcendental reductions have been performed. She assumes Husserl's consent in this, although one might well think that the performance of the reductions for him leaves us with the transcendental ego. Stein takes this to be correct in so far as the transcendental ego includes experience as it

---

specified by the person's personality, allowing the particular person to form community around the values it shares with others.

Ontic structure of the I experiencing	Means of sharing life power, allowing for sociality	Sociality of which the I is capable, given its means of sharing life power	Inter-subjective constitution of which the I is capable
Experiential structure (abilities or faculties)	Common experience	Identifiable experience	'There is another/ someone there'
Psyche	Psychic contagion	Mass	'We sense'
Will	Decision and action	Association	'We have decided'
Person	Value response	Community	'We think'

is experienced. If it does not, there is nothing to investigate and the whole enterprise of phenomenology falls down for lack of material with which to engage. As this is absurd, Stein regards *experience* to be a more accurate description of what is left by the reductions, as indeed I experience not only one I, but several, and could not even conceptualise the I as *an* I (or even as an ego) were it not for the others, nor conceptualise the world were it not for their perspectives on it that allow me to distinguish inter-subjectively constituted objective entities in it. Experience, for Stein, is thus fundamental, it may be shared in various ways, and is as such available for everyone to test, understand, contest and explore. This is how and why phenomenology can be a collaborative enterprise, as envisaged by Husserl.[5]

Experience as we experience it is experienced as motivated. This is so commonplace that we hardly think about the possibility of isolating motivation from experience. Stein defines it thus:

> *Motivation, in our general sense, is the connection that acts get into with one another: (...) an emerging of the one out of the other, a self-fulfilling or being fulfilled of the one on the basis of the other for the sake of the other.*[6]

To Stein motivation is thus not an act, and this makes it unlike perception. It is more on a par with constitution, although motivation must presuppose constitution, as there could be no emerging of one act experienced out of another were it not for entities and acts experienced.[7] On the other hand Stein cannot envisage constitution to be completely inexplicable, and when we explain it, we invariably see it as motivated precisely by its object. Thus the hermeneutical circle is introduced into the heart of intentionality: we

---

5   Husserl might in practice have expected experiential conformity rather than diverse perspectives, differently motivated. This could well be the key to his not considering empathy and inter-subjectivity as decisive as Stein.

6   PPH, I, III, 1, p. 41.

7   Marianne Sawicki discusses the relative importance of empathy, constitution and motivation as regards the phenomenological project in *Body, Text and Science*, Chapter 2 and 3. See also my *On the Problem of Human Dignity. A Hermeneutical and Phenomenological Investigation* (Würzburg: Königshausen und Neumann, 2009), Chapter 9.

interpret what we experience and our motivation in doing so is reflected in what we experience. That we see as we are motivated to see, we see first and foremost in others where it comes to us as the reason for their perspective being different from ours. Having seen it in others, we also see, however, that they see it in us by what Stein calls 'reiterated empathy',[8] and we then conclude that this is how it is: I see the world in a manner that can be explained by (my) motivation.[9]

Turning towards the source of motivation to look at it is a road fraught with difficulties. Partly because it requires the trained ability to empathise, as it is only by means of empathy that values can be seen as objective in the sense of them being something that also exists for others as motivators.[10] If empathy is not sufficiently trained, it is with difficulty that I distinguish motivation from myself: I see its source as if it were identical to me. Then, of course, I cannot explain how it comes about that others are motivated, nor understand what they are motivated by. Thus, insufficiently trained empathy is the first obstacle to overcome when one wants to bring oneself to face the source of motivation. The next is that one might not want to see what one then sees. One might not like to see one's gesture as issuing from jealousy, as this says something about oneself, in which one might not want to recognise oneself. My potential dislike of my jealous self (which again is experienced motivation) shows us something more about values: we experience them as actually informing who we are when we accept the motivation issuing from them as ours. Stein sees them as explaining our personality: our value response as mediated by the psyche's retention of traces of earlier value responses, in turn facilitating others of the same type.[11] Turning our attention to see the source of motivation thus presupposes our trained ability to empathise, which allows us to see the values as objective and not as merely sourced in myself, and our willingness to see ourselves in the light of these values, my values and those of others.[12]

8   PE, 2, 3 (f).
9   Ibid., 3, 5 (g).
10   Ibid., 3, 5 (m–p).
11   Ibid., 4.
12   See also Chapter 12.

But what do we see when we then turn to face the values? The difficulty of seeing what we see quite likely is that we *see* precisely nothing in a literal sense. We see something by insight: we gather information from a myriad of sources to form an intuition of what we see. And then we see 'in images': something like light, life or energy. The most important sources from which we gather this information are feelings, and paired with them our understanding of the state of our psyche that allows us to interpret the information about motivation that the feelings carry.[13]

Let us start with the psyche, to proceed to the feelings and the meaning they carry. The psyche, for Stein, is constituted from all experiences in which life power is experienced as an element.[14] I do not experience the stream of experience to flow always in the same manner: excitement is accompanied by a characteristic artificial quickening of experience, tiredness by the stream 'drying up', so that pain results when one attempts to bring the experiences into a coherent order or understand. Vitality shows up as openness to experiences and a certain ease in bringing them into order. These phenomena are distinct from the experience of motivation because they appear as its limit. Although motivation can feed life power to an extraordinary extent, it cannot produce it. When 'the batteries are flat' as we say, what normally enlivens us becomes a pain, and we may not at all be able to experience it (the mathematical proof, the elegant argument). All we want when entirely exhausted is to switch off the stream of experience, at least to the extent where we have to intervene in it by being conscious. The phenomena of life power hence seems to testify to something that is not motivation, to the type of causality which Stein calls 'psychic

13   Ibid., 3.
14   Ibid. and PPH, I. Stein seems to be the only one among the phenomenologists to have elaborated a distinction between psyche and spirit. As a consequence understanding of the emotions allows her to see them as analysable as psychic phenomena with a physical as well as a spiritual side. See Christof Betschart, 'Was ist Lebenskraft? Edith Steins erkenntnistheoretischen Prämissen in "Psychische Kausalität" (Teil 1)' in *Edith Stein Jahrbuch* 2009, pp. 154–84; and 'Was ist Lebenskraft? Edith Steins anthropologischer Beitrag in "Psychische Kausalität" (Teil 2)' in *Edith Stein Jahrbuch* 2010, pp. 33–64.

causality', which cannot be infelt or understood but can nevertheless be observed as part of 'nature'.[15]

The experience of life power allows us to constitute the psyche as a characteristic of 'me', as something that colours 'my' experiences, in the same way as someone else's psyche colours the experiences of him or her. The psyche however, does not form part of the spiritual world of values that I experience as motivating my own person and that of others; it is experienced as transcendent, as pertaining to me or him because we are also embedded in a causal network which is different from that of the spirit. The law of this network of nature is causality, just like the law of the network that is spirit is motivation.[16]

Having seen what the psyche is, we can start looking at the feelings. They are experienced as pertaining to both networks, that of nature and that of the spirit: they cause something in me (the blood to rush, the hands to sweat, the knees to weaken) and they are motivated by something that comes to me as a message sounding something like 'this is valuable', 'dangerous', 'horrid', 'beautiful'.[17] The message carried is the motivating power of

---

15   PPH, I. 'If I feel myself to be weary, then the current of life seems to stagnate, as it were. It creeps along sluggishly, and everything that's occurring in the different sensory fields is involved in it. The colours are sort of colourless, the tones are hollow, and every "impression" – each datum that is registered with the life stream against its will, so to speak – is painful, unpleasant. Every colour, every tone, every touch "hurts". If the weariness subsides, then a shift enters the other spheres as well. And the moment when the weariness changes into vigour, the current starts to pump briskly, it surges forward unrestrainedly. Everything that is emerging in it carries the whiff of vigour and joyfulness' (pp. 14–15).

16   Ibid., I, V. Husserl's *Ideas II* is based on the same idea, and it is worth remarking, that Stein wrote PPH immediately after having taken her leave as Husserl's assistant, during which period she among other things edited *Ideas II* and *III*.

17   PE, 4, 1: 'All outer perception is carried out in spiritual acts. Similarly, in every literal act of empathy, i.e. in every comprehension of an act of feeling, we have already penetrated into the realm of the spirit. For, as physical nature is constituted in perceptual acts, so a new object realm is constituted in feeling. This is the world of values. In joy the subject has something joyous facing him, in fright something frightening, in fear something threatening. Even moods have their objective correlate. For him who is cheerful, the world is bathed in a rosy glow; for him who is depressed,

what is intended. What I feel is where it can carry me; who I'll be if I let it into the substance of my soul; what can happen as a result of this power. My psyche lights up at the message, depending on how it is prepared to receive it, and the spiritual energy reverberates through it like sound through a musical instrument. The psyche is the sounding board, which transforms spiritual energy into causal phenomena and make me feel physically what otherwise is invisible and does not belong to the world of nature at all. The psyche is the antenna that captures the signal, the network that stores the message; the feeling is the act in which I detect this physical reaction, this fluctuation in life power, caused by the spiritual energy passing through. Just like it is possible for me to disengage from my field of vision (if I am concentrating on what someone is saying, for example, or am listening to music), I can disengage from the field of emotions, thus paying no attention to the information carried in them, if I want to concentrate on another source of information, say what can be seen or heard or known about an object apart from its value. Some people think that science is made this way, and only in this way, that science per definition is 'value free', i.e. disconnected from things value. To Stein such an idea would beg for completion, as the whole question of the motivation for such science is left unexplored. It would by its own inner necessity lead to a discussion of the driving interest, of social paradigms setting an agenda behind the back of the scientists, and ultimately to a discussion of the entire social setting that makes the science meaningful as activity for the scientists, investors and society at large. Science is, according to Stein, 'objective', that is appropriately addressing its object, only when it takes all factors relating to this object into account, and that includes its value, as any object is only ever completely constituted when it is constituted also in its value.

---

bathed in black. And all this is co-given with acts of feeling as belonging to them. It is primarily appearances of expression that grant us access to these experiences. As we consider expressions to be proceeding from experiences, we have the spirit here simultaneously reaching into the physical world, the spirit "becoming visible" in the living body. This is made possible by the psychic reality of acts as experiences of a psycho-physical individual, and it involves an effect on spiritual nature' (p. 92).

Feelings are therefore far from irrelevant in science, in particular in the humanities, where the information they carry is at the centre of the investigation. We already designated them as a kind of physical measure of the effect of spiritual energy on the psyche. Like the mercury that rises in the thermometer indicates heat in the surroundings because mercury expands, anger is felt in the blood rushing to the back of the brow and the tension of the body preparing for aggression. Love is felt in the inclination of the heart, the loosening of the limbs, the easy acceptance of the presence of the other in close proximity. With them feelings carry the message: this makes me angry, I love that person: the object they present to us has the formal quality (as Aquinas would say) of being 'uneasily avoidable evil' or 'good' and hence reveal to us a valuation we have always already performed when we feel.[18] The first things with which attention to feelings thus confronts us is this implicit valuation, over which in fact I experience myself as having much more control than over the feelings, which are sheer reactions, affects, effects of spiritual energy on the psyche. The valuation is the allowance I make for the effect to proceed into my action: I do think this attitude, act, situation is bad, and I therefore allow myself to be angry; I do think this person is lovely, therefore I allow myself to love him or her. If I do not value this attitude positively, then I revise my attitude. I then don't allow the anger to flow freely; it is cut at its source, so to speak, since I think there is nothing to be angry about. Likewise with the love: if the person turns out not to be lovely at all, the love dries up at the source or must find another source from which to flow. The situation is different if I feel the anger, and feel it is justified, but know that it is socially inexpedient to express it, and take this as my motive for not expressing the anger. Then the anger is still there, still motivating me, just like the love might be, even when it cannot find an acceptable expression.

The feelings make me realise the presence of the motivation as it reaches the level of detectability in the psyche. I retain the possibility of taking an attitude in relation to them, i.e. stand over them and let the motivation they carry determine my actions or in contrast, not allow their energy to

18 *Summa theologiae* Ia IIae, q. 25, a. 4.

determine the direction of my motivation as an acting person.[19] This is what I achieve by means of the act of valuation.[20]

The objectivity of values

Having looked at the feelings as a source of information about the values for psycho-physical persons, we must proceed to look at what it is we gain insight into by means of feelings. The experience of not wanting the feeling felt to determine one's actions implies in fact that we have another, more direct way of accessing and thus experiencing motivation, which is not

19   PPH, I, III, § 3–4: 'I can "take a stance" towards the attitude, in a new sense. I can accept it, plant my feet on it, and declare my allegiance to it. Suppose I accept it – that means that if it emerges in me I give myself over to it, joyously, without reluctance. Suppose I deny it – that doesn't mean I eliminate it. That's not under my control. "Cancelling out" a belief would require new motives, through which the motives of the original belief are invalidated and from which the cancellation is established instead "all by itself". But I need not acknowledge this belief. I can comport myself just as though it were not present; I can make it inoperative. (It is this, the comporting, that Husserl designated as *epochē*. The acts rendered inoperative are "neutralised")' (p. 49).

20   It cannot be said that Stein developed an ethics or a moral philosophy, although there is the basis for doing so in her writings on anthropology on the one hand and her value theory on the other. The difficulties of unifying phenomenology and Aristotelianism are broached by John Drummond in his 'Aristotelianism and Phenomenology' published in the work edited by him cited above, pp. 15–45. Judith Parsons' thesis: *Edith Stein: Toward an Ethic of Relationship and Responsibility,* Duquesne University 2005 could be a starting point for such an investigation. It could be argued that education theory, because education is a moral act par excellence, implicitly contain an ethics or moral philosophy. See also: Bernhard Augustin, 'Ethische Elemente in der Anthropologie Edith Steins' in *Die unbekannte Edith Stein: Phänomenologie und Sozialphilosophie,* ed. by Beckmann-Zöller and Gerl-Falkovitz (New York: Peter Lang, 2006), pp. 193–200. The article is based on a doctoral dissertation of the same name.

dependent on bodily feeling. If I deny myself the right to be angry facing an object I cannot really want to condemn or regard as bad, it is because I 'see' that it is not so bad after all, that compared to others, say, it comes out rather well, that its effects have proven acceptable, that others have benefited from it, etc. By reasoning I compute the potential effects of the motivating power in order to evaluate it 'objectively', i.e. according to what it is in itself. When all is counted I judge that it is after all not worth being angry about. This ability to compute motivation from various sources and refer it back to itself brings the value into focus. We rely on this ability when we reason. When I add 2 + 2 I focus the value of 2, i.e. its motivating power, and I add it to 2 to get the motivating power of 4. Logic, as Husserl also thought, has the same fundamental structure as axiology; to Stein this is the case because both rely on the ability to estimate motivating power.

This computing, however, does not happen at the same pace in everyone.[21] Like some have specific talents for mathematics, others have specific 'emotional intelligence' or depth of interpretation, and hence we teach each other and learn from each other. Education is a systematic effort to bring values to the attention of the child growing up and to the adult in quest of deeper knowledge. 'Moral education' is specifically addressed at forming the character of the individual and is therefore of particular importance for the individual and to society at large. It addresses the question of what values to prefer to others, which is always already raised by the fact that I can take an attitude in relation to my feelings and sometimes feel I must do that. Since I feel that the value motivating my attitude is higher than the one revealing itself in my emotions, I form a value hierarchy. That means I place one value as more important than another, or recognise in one value a higher motivating power than in another.

In this process I can get confused by the fact that I can access motivating power in two indirect ways. I can access it by means of the psyche

---

21 I know this by the means of empathy as explained above, and in general my ability to empathise gives much more scope to my experience of values, partly because it allows me to access values I did not know about otherwise and partly because it allows me to constitute the values as objective, i.e. as there for others as well.

being 'contaminated' with it as it is transferred from one psychic network to another.[22] I can also access motivational power by decision, in which case my willpower will interfere with my ability to measure the motivating power of the values.[23] As we grow up these relationships are not transparent to us, and we don't always know wherefrom our motivation stems, whether from the expectations of my family, tribe or peers, or the power structures of the state in which I am raised. But that there are deeper or higher values is testified to by the fact that we do reflect on our motivation and do not like to be deceived, even by ourselves. There also are *a priori* relationships between the values, which might help me reasoning about them. A higher value must be preferred to a lower one, for example, or the existence of a negative value is itself of negative value, for example.[24] Many accounts exist of what the highest values are, and we learn about them as we grow up (i.e. different religions, ideologies, movements). We might commit ourselves to some of them, by valuing them as our own values and thus measuring in our own life their motivating power. We also learn from the motivating power we see values having in other people's life. It is this motivating power we can have insight into, since the values *are their motivating power* of which we always have expandable experience.

---

22   This happens when individuals form a mass, as at a football match, a rock concert or a mass political meeting. PPH, II, II, §4 (b). Dancers, lovers, sportsmen and physical workers learn to make use of this psychic unification. We can also form psychical unities with animals, as the rider does with his horse, or the dog or falcon does with the hunter. Scheler mentions emotional infection (*The Nature of Sympathy* (London: Routledge and Keegan Paul, 1954), and no doubt Stein is inspired by him in her account. He does not however systematically distinguish psyche and spirit.

23   PPH, II, II, §4 (c).

24   James H. Smith, *Wert, Rechtheit* and *Gut. Adolph Reinach's Contribution to Early Phenomenological Ethics*. Doctoral dissertation, National University of Ireland, Maynooth (now: University of Maynooth), 2013.

The importance of values for who we are

That we know about values allows us to know that we are persons, as persons are subjects that experience themselves as value-related, as motivated.[25] This is not all we are, as we are not exclusively spiritual: we are also of the type of psycho-physical individual which is called a human being.[26] We are human persons, not angels, not gods, not animals, not things, but have something in common with all of these: The fact that we are persons with angels and God, the fact that we have a psyche with animals, and the fact that we have a physical body in the world with things.

Knowledge about values also allows us to know that our value response forms our personality. Personality seems to have a depth dimension linked to the soul, since I experience the level of depth of soul at which my personal value response allows me to express myself in my actions, corresponding to the height of the motivating power of the values accessed.[27] The personality is the structure that allows for this response (or indeed precludes it), such that it is what allows the soul to find expression (or not). Personality is thus the filter that allows me to be who I truly am or indeed what prevents me from being it.

***

Stein's phenomenological investigation of value is based on experience being both personal and shared by means of empathy. It develops an intuition that was already present in Husserl, but did not unfold because of the undeveloped nature of his theory of empathy and his consequent understanding of transcendentally reduced experience. Stein in contrast sees constitution itself as motivated and thus introduces hermeneutics

---

25 PE, 4, 2.
26 PE conducts constitutional analyses of the psychophysical individual and the spiritual person (Chapter 3 and 4 respectively). This analysis is continued in *Einführung* and *Aufbau*.
27 PE, 4, 3.

into the phenomenological analysis in a manner that allows us to see all experience, all constitution, as motivated and therefore interpretable. As such this type of phenomenology of value and motivation could be of significance to all sciences which investigate worldview dependent topics, in particular sociology, politics, law, history, anthropology and literature.

CHAPTER 4

The Motivated Constitution of the State

Stein's *Philosophy of Psychology and the Humanities*, written immediately after Stein took her leave as Husserl's assistant, were meant to complement Husserl's *Ideas II* in respect of the constitution of the psyche and the spirit.[1] Stein's doctoral dissertation *On the Problem of Empathy* equipped her well for this task, as the complete constitution of both the psyche and the spirit depends on the mirror perspective offered by the other, accessed by means of empathy. The access to the experience of the other allows me to identify the world of values – the objects of motivation – as objective, and to understand myself as a being whose nature stands under the influence of the motivation which my I is subject to as a person, and also to identify myself as a sentient being in possession of a psyche. Her understanding of mental energy allows her to analyse the formation of the 'we' which arises from the sharing of motivational energy and gives rise to communal experience. With the understanding of the flexible formation of the communal subject a map of the dynamic structure of inter-subjectivity is achieved, and with it, as its correlate, an understanding of the inter-subjective constitution of the world; a model of what could be called its 'social construction'.

It is the community-forming ability of values that make them of decisive importance for Stein's concept of the state, as the state is a community or at least relies on community. To explain this we must start by (1) accounting for the systematic relationship that obtains between personality and community according to Stein and (2) discuss the relationship between personality and the various types of sociality: mass, association

---

1   Ideas II and III were not, however, published during Stein's lifetime: she had expected that they would have been published a short time after her own PPH.

and community. We can then (3) discuss the state in relation to these types and the motivation for its constitution.

Personality and community

Only persons are capable of community. *En revanche* persons are *essentially* capable of community.[2] This is so because the person is constituted from the I's value-relatedness and because a person, by being capable of accessing motivational energy from values, can share this energy provided by the values with other persons.[3]

Whereas a person is capable of spiritual life, a personality stands before us as already motivated and hence as a source of a specific type of motivation. That it is already motivated in this manner means that the values which motivate it shape or determine it, producing a relatively permanent tendency towards striving for their realisation. This determination means that it is prone to form community with those whose values it shares, and who consequently have a similar personality structure. Many of our character and personality traits remain unnoticed by us, and may be revealed only in situations where we are not in our habitual surroundings. What makes our specificity inconspicuous is the fact that we often share our traits with those around us, with people from our community. Only when we encounter persons who do not display these traits do we notice them. We tend to share them with those around us because values, as objective, are publicly available and can motivate many persons for the same objective. Those around us tend to discover what we value and why, or simply

2   'Where a subject accepts the other as a subject and does not confront him but rather lives with him and is determined by the stirrings of his life, they are forming a community with one another. [...] In the community solidarity prevails.' PPH II, Introduction, p. 130.

3   PE, IV.

to share our values by loyalty or sentient contagion, and therefore tend to value the same things as we do. Values draw persons into a relationship of co-motivatedness, which is experienced as a unity that allows for the co-ordination of actions.[4] When reflected upon, this unity is understood to be the basis for what we call community. Community arises from the experience of being already organised by one's subjective initiative and personal creativity (i.e. by one's personality) into larger overlapping realities of 'likeminded' people, i.e. of people engaged in realising the same values as one self. These persons share mental life-power with each other and consequently experience themselves as being able to say 'we', i.e. pertain to the same super-individual subject.

Personality and other forms of sociality

Whereas similar experiential structure is the precondition for the experience of sociality, sentient contagion and association constitutes two further ways of sharing mental energy apart from community.[5] In the case of sentient contagion the energy is transmitted directly from one psyche to the other, without intentionality involving value-response on the part of the contaminated individual. This individual is being energised from the energy of someone else, without being aware that the source of the motivation he is acting on belongs to someone else. In this manner he forms a super-individual entity with this other (or these others), who themselves may or may not have knowledge of the source of the motivation in question.

In association, by contrast, the value response is decided upon in a kind of commitment brought about by an act of will, and the choice therefore need not accurately reflect the spontaneous value-response of the individual. It nevertheless makes his value-allegiance public and (relatively)

---

4   Jürgen Habermas: *The Inclusion of the Other*, p. 3 ff.
5   See Chapter 3, note 4 for a schematic representation.

predictable, and it in principle involves some knowledge of the values to which a commitment is made. Here the energy from the values to the realisation of which one is committed through membership of the association (the party, the society, the institution) might not be directly accessed and hence the values chosen might not be appreciated in their full motivating power (whether positive or negative). This means that the personality of the member of the association might not accurately (or indeed at all) reflect the values the association is formed to promote.

Of community, in contrast, personality is an accurate reflection. This is because the community relies on the sharing of energy issuing from values that community members experience personally. These values are perhaps not conscious in the sense that persons can list them or name them, but they are conscious in the sense that if they are named and explained, the person will be able to identify himself as motivated by them. Others see this motivation as expressing itself in the personality of the community member.

The different ways in which I am motivated, by sentient contagion, loyalty or personal value response, hence show in my personality. That I am open to sentient contagion shows up as suggestibility and a certain vagueness of character making me susceptible to sway in various directions, for no reason other than the mood of the crowd. The suggestible person has a somewhat unfinished character, as we see it in children. The associational commitment of a person shows up as loyalty to certain defined purposes or people expressing certain values whether or not they are his own. What someone does out of loyalty shows something about the character the person wants to have, or accepts to have, about what he has chosen to be part of.

These distinctions are so familiar to us that we often overlook the experiences that allow us to identify them. The merit of Stein's value theory is to explicate our over-familiar intuitions: how we read motivations from people's behaviour and characters and how we conclude to their relationships with others from what we see of these motivations. The subtle and necessary understanding of who we are in relation to our surroundings relies on these intuitions, which indeed we sometimes resist explicating for fear of what we might see.

It remains that a personality, as it concretises the person's value response, *ipso facto* aligns a person to other persons motivated by the same values. This relation constitutes the possibility of the community that might arise as a concrete unity involving an overlap of many different value responses. Association is commitment to community and sentient contagion a shortcut to it, which in fact also cuts the person short of his own personal value response and may alternately relieve him or stifle him. The person, thus, is involved by its essence in communities corresponding to its personality so that the social reflects the individual and the individual the social reality of the person.

The state as community and association

The analogy that exists between the individual person and the super-individual agent, which Stein treats of in *Individual and Community*, allows her to compare the relationship between personality and person with the relationship between community and state.[6] Like the personality is determining spontaneity and giving specificity to the person, so the nation provides content and direction to the state. The state whose essence is sovereignty combined with being the source of positive law and independent government provides a default unity allowing for supra-individual action, in the same manner as the transcendental unity of the personal I allows for the will to act on behalf of the individual, mostly in accordance with the person's personality. In the individual person, the person is the source of the unity of the personality, but on the supra-individual level this relationship is reversed: the state does not confer unity upon the community underlying it; this unity is in contrast provided by its own cultural creativity. The state seems to endure better if it confirms an already existing cultural unity, and in this sense it relies for its life on the life of the community of

6   PPH, II.

which it is the organising principle. The person endures, even if it acts in a manner that is totally out of character, but it does endure better if it acts in accordance with its personality or with laws that explains its development. The community may exist without the state: in Poland and Ireland for example, national communities existed for centuries without a state to express them. A personality, in contrast, cannot exist independently of the person whose personality it is even in fictional characters, as we cannot imagine these without them belonging to fictional persons. In this manner an individual person is experienced as being presupposed or founding as it constitutes itself, whereas the super-individual agent which is the state is affirming itself by its power. The state constitutes itself as sovereign and expresses this self constitution in its legislation, but from below it is constituted by its citizens in a manner that prepares or allows for this agency, in particular by their obedience and promulgation of the laws issuing from it.[7]

How and why, do we constitute the state? Not all people do, and some – anarchists – think one ought not to. Most people do it because the community needs to be able to act as one, and therefore tends towards constituting itself as a state, i.e. towards positing its own sovereignty in terms of which it legislates and governs itself. With the state positive law emerges. But the state does not necessarily presuppose a community. Its affirmation of power can rise out of a single man's ambition, or out of a certain class' desire to rule. The state may also accommodate several communities, but then it does not serve the purpose of enabling *a* community to act on its own behalf; then it can only act for several communities at the same time, something that may or may not be to the advantage of these communities. These considerations explain the relative stability and meaningfulness of the nation state, and the peculiar hollowness that can be observed in states that have been constructed by power alone (whether dynastic, imperial, colonial or other). If we cannot act as 'us' we cannot attribute meaning to acting collectively, and the state then becomes largely irrelevant. This 'us' may be formed by community (in which case it is strong and conscious), by

7   See Andreas Lukas, 'Recht und Staat bei Edith Stein', in the *Edith Stein Jahrbuch* 2014, pp. 92–110 for a serious engagement with Stein's theory of law.

association (in which case it is chosen, whether reluctantly or enthusiastically) or by sentient contagion (in which case it is transferred and expresses motivation in principle foreign to the person and therefore ultimately volatile). The strength of the state relies on the amount of people who let themselves be determined by its sovereignty to determine it as their 'we'. It relies in other words on the number or proportion of people within the community or communities over which the state extends its sovereignty that value the ability to act as a super-individual agent by means of it, whether these people value this agency directly or have committed themselves to it by choice, or indeed have contracted the valuation from others, whether parents, superiors or peers. It remains that some must value the agency to set the standard for those who commit themselves to the value, and to provide the mental energy for contagion of those who are motivated by sentient contagion.

Many of the initiatives in which we are involved depend on the state for their stability. This is why valuing any of these involve one in valuing the state as a means to realise these. Stein therefore claims that for the state to emerge, the community needs to be marked by a high degree of organisational (associational) activity.[8]

There are thus two ways in which the state can be weakened: by weakening the community that underlies the state, and by weakening the will to value the ability to act as a super-individual *in this manner* (whether because the community is split, its initiative is made redundant by spontaneous peace and harmony or because other forms of super-individual initiatives have taken over).

***

To Stein the state is not by itself good, i.e. it is not part of its essence that it is beneficial to those who constitute it, whether subjects or outsiders. It is in contrast part of the essence of the state that it is sovereign. It is power, simply, and as such empty of content. The need to maintain sovereignty in a changing world means the state has a tendency to eliminate

---

8   State, I, §3, c.

forms of order that are not its own. Whatever challenges its sovereignty, it must experience as a potential danger. For this reason it is up to those who constitute the communities underlying the state, and in particular to those of these communities who come to represent the state by acting as the representatives of the community, to ensure that the state is harnessed to positive values. The state is not able by itself to discern such values, nor to realise them, but the community can, because individual persons can.

The social construction of the state relies on our valuation of the ability to act in common. It in turn is dependent on the existence of a community that gives sense to acting in common. This community does not have to be a nation. It could be religious, ideological, commercial or indeed universal. Because community essentially expresses the person, the ultimate community seems to have to correspond to who we really are. This is why Stein moves on in her later career to consider the question of who, and what, the human being is as such. She comes to see this question as fundamental to both social and political philosophy and therefore no longer needs to discuss these. *An Investigation Concerning the State* is therefore conclusive of a chapter in her life. The phenomenological understanding of our ability to affect the inter-subjective constitution of the world, however, is to underpin all her later philosophy.

CHAPTER 5

An Analysis of Human Dignity *pace* Stein

Human dignity is a term it is not easy to define, even though most of us will make use of the term now and then. Nor is it a reality that is easy to describe precisely, although it seems to be something of which we all have a keen intuition and which matters to us in a vital way. In what follows I shall propose a definition that allows us to describe the intuition of human dignity by means of Stein's phenomenology.

Addressing the topic of human dignity according to the phenomenology of Edith Stein requires a preliminary comment about Stein's own idea of human dignity and the relationship it bears with our present analysis. Stein did not explicitly write on human dignity, nor did it interest her specifically to give an account of what it is, although the reality probably mattered as much to her as to anyone of us. She lived and wrote before the expression found its lasting form in the human rights tradition, but had she survived the Second World War, it is likely she would have found this development of particular interest. However, Stein used the corresponding German expression *Menschenwürde* three times in her work. In her autobiography *Life in a Jewish Family* she explains her own life long abstention from alcohol by reference to human dignity.[1] In *Potency and Act* she explains her own emphasis on the individuality of the human being with reference to human dignity.[2] And in *Was ist der Mensch?* she describes human dignity as what intrinsically limits the desire for power and status.[3] These three uses testify to an understanding of human dignity which sees it as a call to autonomy, as a good possessed by every human individual,

---

1   I, 4; p. 47.
2   VI, 23, h, p. 395.
3   I, C, p. 13.

and as the ultimate foundation of justice. Such an understanding is both common and current.[4] It is moreover in accordance with the developments we shall make.

As Stein, however, did not develop her specific understanding of human dignity any further, it is not Stein's philosophy of human dignity we shall explore in what follows. It is, in contrast, what it is possible to say about human dignity, given her understanding of phenomenology. Her understanding of phenomenology is special because of its emphasis on the motivated constitution of objects and on the intelligibility of objects presenting themselves for our interpretation in 'types'. We shall talk about human dignity 'according to' it, because Stein's special version of phenomenology is well suited to think about and properly identify human dignity.

Recently Sarah Borden Sharkey has expressed a worry that Stein's thought would not allow for a conceptualisation of human equality and dignity because Stein understands the individual to be the carrier of the species form and not the reverse, as Aquinas does.[5] Borden Sharkey is right that the species form is understood by the later Stein to be attributed to the human being by virtue of its individual essence, and also right that this makes Stein's position differ from Aquinas'.[6] That the individual has an essence, for Stein, does not however mean that it does not also, as part of this essence, pertain to the human race of which there is also an essence (which the individual human being therefore also 'has'), and that this being, as a consequence, is of the human 'type'. The fact that an individual pertains to different types by virtue of its essential features is understood by Borden Sharkey, as well as by Stein, to be an advantage the notion of 'type' has over the notion of species, given the difficulties raised for this latter notion by Darwin's theory of evolution.[7] But while the epistemological function of the type is the same as that of the logical notion of 'species', it

---

4   For a history of the notion of human dignity see Lebech, *On the Problem of Human Dignity*, Part I.

5   Sarah Borden Sharkey, *Thine Own Self. Individuality in Edith Stein's Later Writings* (Washington DC: University of America Press, 2010).

6   We shall discuss this in Chapters 9 and 10.

7   Aufbau, I, V, II, 1.

does not *per se* exclude that the individual belongs to other types as well, which may be more or less essential to it.[8] Borden Sharkey misunderstands this interpretative function of the type,[9] as does also Sawicki to whom she refers for support in her criticism.[10] Taking our point of departure in Stein's early phenomenology, we shall show how it is also in virtue of its particular understanding of type, that Stein's phenomenology allows us to explain what is involved in our intuition of human dignity, and that therefore far from being an offence against human dignity, this notion in fact is of particular value, when we attempt to understand it.

In the following we shall further outline Stein's phenomenological description of value (1). Then we shall see how the human being 'comes together for us', i.e. we shall conduct a 'constitutional analysis' of the human being, to whom fundamental value might be attributed (2). And finally we shall show how it comes about that we identify this being, the human being (the being of the human type), as being a being of *fundamental* value, i.e. as of a value that cannot be dispensed with without the coherence of human experience itself fragmenting (3).

Stein's account of value and motivation

It is possibly the fact that values often are taken to be perspective dependent that has left them outside the pale of scientific investigation. From a phenomenological standpoint however, values can be investigated precisely for what we take them to be. For Stein, and this marks her distinctive approach, I learn about values from the motivational energy I experience

8   See also Chapter 8.
9   Borden Sharkey: *Thine Own Self*, pp. 179–84.
10 Sawicki: *Body Text and Science*, pp. 181–3.

them to have, under the two-fold perspective of experiencing it directly myself and experiencing others experiencing it, by means of empathy.[11]

Motivational energy is a complex phenomenon, involving both psychic causality and pure (spiritual) motivation. These two dimensions of the concrete experience of value in fact form the formal objects of Psychology (the psyche) and the Humanities (*Geist* understood as motivatedness), such that the experience of value is legitimately studied by both, albeit under different aspects. The distinction between the psyche and the spirit relies on the distinction between life-power and motivation; life-power being the causal factor in our experiences, which makes us experience the stream of consciousness as flowing gently, drying up or rushing violently at us,[12] and motivation being the meaningful process of proceeding from reasons and values into which one may gain insight.[13]

We identify motivation by means of values, but the motivation is felt as positive or negative depending on the enlivening or deadening influence it has on our life in its entirety.[14] Although there may be a direct insight into (or feeling of) value besides its effect on our emotional life, feeling mostly influences our psycho-physical 'space' and registers in it as having a psycho-physical component. In so far as values are felt through the prism of the psyche, the effect of the motivating power that we feel depends not only on the motivating power of the values themselves but also on the condition of the psyche, in its turn standing under the influence of the body, the physical environment, and the shape we impose on both by our actions.

As we value differently, i.e. prefer the motivational power of some values above others in different ways, we also are affected by this energy in different, albeit comparable, ways. That is why we can learn about values from others and be surprised by the power they have in them, and so revise

---

11   'Now as for the egoic contents [of affective acts], they have a twofold constitutive function. One, they are the material on the basis of which values come to givenness for us. And two, they deliver up the stuff for the corresponding affective attitude.' PPH, p. 160.

12   PPH, I, II.

13   PE, IV, 1–2; pp. 91–7.

14   PPH, II, I, § 2, c), pp. 157–65.

our value hierarchies, which are expressing themselves in our character and personality.[15] A higher value is one that has a higher motivating power, i.e. can motivate in situations where other values fail to provide reasons for action, and is consequently a value I ought to prefer to other, lower, values. It lies in the nature of valuation that I cannot be caused to accomplish it, that preferring a higher value to a lower is a free, motivated act, which I accomplish because I think it should be accomplished, or because I want to accomplish it. It also lies in the nature of valuation that I may be mistaken about what is of highest value: this may in fact show itself not to have the motivating power I thought it had, and this experience might occasion that I revise my value hierarchy.

Motivational energy is felt in feelings, but it is also observable in the stance I take in relation to these and in my free action realising the motivating values in the world. Hence actions, and their products, institutions, and other cultural objects express the values they realise. When I read these values in the cultural world, I get to understand what motivates the society for whom they are meaningful. Thus spirit is expressed objectively in the cultural world as well as experienced as subjective.[16]

The experience of a particular value (i.e. of a particular type of motivation) is often conceptually identified by us by means of the bearer of the value and/or the type of community it animates, such as in 'the value of gold' (here gold identifies the value) or 'conservative values' (here the community of conservatives identify the value). The value can also be described in terms of the 'height' it occupies in the value hierarchy; but this is not a marker that allows me to identify it to others who place the value at a different level, *except* if we are talking about a 'dignity', which *in principle* means a fundamental value, a highest value from which other values derive their value.

15　PE, IV, 7 (b).
16　Einführung, II, d), 3, e; PE, p. 92: 'Our whole "cultural world", all that the "hand of man" has formed, all utilitarian objects, all works of handicraft, applied science and art are the reality correlative to spirit.'

The fact that I place my values in a hierarchy stems from the fact that I have to act on them and thus must choose between them, and also from the fact that some values are dependent on others for their realisation. The choices I make coalesce to form my character. In the process of deciding what to place higher and act upon, I not only think about foundational relationships between values, but I can also look to others to see what they have done in a similar situation, ask them 'what they think' or read what they feel from their expression. In this manner, I form an understanding that such and such a type would value in such and such a manner, and thereby also of what type of person I am, in my own eyes and in those of others. It is also possible to absorb directly from the psyches of others the motivational response of my surroundings, either consciously because I form a community with them, or unconsciously through psychic contagion. Psychic contagion per definition has not passed through the filter of personal value response or choice, but it mimics the personal value response of the person who chooses to live in community and thus respond to the values of those with whom she or he lives.[17] Psychic contagion, as the expression states, affects me directly through the psyche, so that I become infected by motivational energy I have not chosen to value. This registers in the value hierarchy visible in my personality as suggestibility or weakness of character.

Because we act, we cannot avoid forming a value hierarchy, and thus we constantly make decisions affecting our character and personality by preferring one value to another. We have to live with who we are in our own eyes, and with what others think of us, and thus we necessarily have a relationship to the world of values. This usually spurs us to think and argue about what we want to place highest, both on the personal level and in our communities. Our discussions with or among ourselves presuppose that there is something that is better, and thus testifies to the fact that values form an objective hierarchy among themselves, a hierarchy that we can access and normatively assess because we can gain insight into it. Hence, by saying that the value of the human being is *fundamental*, one claims that it

17   Ibid. II, I, § 3, c), pp. 175–90.

ought to be valued highest by all, that is *should* be preferred to every other value, that other values are derived from it, and thus that it is objectively higher than any other value.

The constitution of the human being

So who or what is this human being to whom such fundamental value might be attributed?

The phenomenological starting point adopted by Stein brackets transcendent reality together with all theoretical constructions so as to retain only experience as it is experienced. Notice, however, that experience as we experience it still includes the experience of others who, like ourselves, experience themselves to be human beings. What makes us identify them (and ourselves) as human, according to Stein?

The first thing characteristic of other human beings is that I see them as experiencing in the same way as I experience myself; they are Is; other Is. An I is the pole of all experience, accompanying every experience, even the ones I have of other Is experiencing. Because I, in these experiences, experience another I experiencing, I gain another perspective on myself, namely as another might experience it. I experience this other experiencing me and a comparison of perspectives is inaugurated which is the normal environment in which I learn to identify things and name them. It is part of this normal environment that I understand myself and the other to be also motivated. I refer to the subjectivity of the I, in so far as it is consciously motivated and performing one act because of another, as a person. The other, who is like me, is experienced as a person, because I experience myself as such, i.e. experience myself to be motivated.

Turning from the other to my own lived experience, I experience around my zero point of orientation a peculiarly structured field from which I cannot walk away, in the way I can walk away from other things. This field is a field of continuous experiencing in the sense that I experience throughout it (e.g., a pain in the stomach, lightness in the head), but I also experience it 'from without' in that I can see and touch it, although not every part of it. Some parts of the body (for this continuous field of experience is my lived body) always 'turn away from me' and can only be seen by me by means of a mirror. In this way I partly experience my body as a thing among other things in the world. It is both sensing and sensed and it is also 'where' I experience emotions involving bodily sensations: the sinking of the grieving heart, the heat of the rushing blood, the light-headedness of exuberant joy.

The body is experienced as having a form, i.e. as ending in a surface that is sensitive to an 'outside', and also as possessing senses located in par-ticular places, each opening up a different field of access to the world, fields of vision, hearing, tasting, sensation. The subject of these senses does not quite seem to be the body, however, as experiencing by means of them is not quite taking up space like the body is. Their subject is rather the *soul*, which takes in their information to process it and forms an interior space of a different quality compared to physical space, a place of depth and sense.

I learn to identify my body as objective, i.e. as perceivable by others, in the same movement as I learn to identify the body of the other I as pecu-liarly his or hers. I experience us both as having a zero point of orientation, wherefrom our worlds extend. My body is grouped around this point from which I cannot move away, just like your body is grouped around your zero point of orientation. Just as I feel my face stretching into a characteristic expression we call a smile, I see the stretching on your face and empathi-cally 'feel my way into it', and to what motivates it, just like I 'feel my way into' what motivates my own smile. Thus the body is also the place for the expression of motivational energy, as a kind of extension of the fact that sensations and emotions are felt throughout it. Moreover, in expression, a certain offloading of the motivational energy is experienced, as motiva-tion tends towards realisation. The type of expressivity I understand as mine, together with the type of body and soul which render it possible, allows me to identify as the type of being that I am, a human being, and this identification simultaneously identifies my 'others', i.e. those whose experience I take to be like mine and hence to co-constitute my (inter-subjective) world. There might be other intelligent beings with a different body structure; there might be intelligent beings without a body: both would differ significantly from the type of being I am: an experiencing bodily being of the human type or kind.

The constitution of the fundamental value of the human being

It is because we constitute ourselves as human beings, i.e. identify ourselves as of the type of beings which we refer to as human, that other human beings matter to us as our 'others', and that indeed all other human beings matter to us in this way. But what exactly is the value of the human being to us? Does it vary from person to person? In situations of war, and in particular in situations involving genocide, it shocks us how little fellow human beings can matter to each other. But then we are precisely that, shocked. We react as if something is amiss when faced with disrespect for human beings. If faced with having to accept it for political reasons, we tend to call it something else: 'neutralisation of the enemy' or 'population management'. It seems to be impossible for us to accept that human beings could be, without it being *wrong* (in whatever way we understand that), treated as if they were not human beings.

This is because our whole experience is built up inter-subjectively, relying on the normal interchangeability of perspectives between the I and the other I, and because we have learnt to understand ourselves as human beings first and foremost, i.e. learnt to identify ourselves as human beings; interpret ourselves according to the type of the human being with its various components, and understand 'our others', who are most like us, to be, first and foremost, human.

In so far as the notion of 'type' plays this pivotal role of identifying our human others (and hence identify those to whom human dignity is or should be attributed), it is remarkable that both Sawicki and Borden Sharkey, despite their otherwise opposed perspectives on Stein, should agree that Stein's use of this notion of 'type' is somehow an affront to human dignity.[18]

The reason for this misunderstanding might be linked to the idea that the human being could be reduced to its type, in particular to its type of personality, an idea Stein herself regards as an affront to human dignity in the passage from *Potency and Act* referred to at the beginning of this chapter. But although 'type' is a notion Stein inherits from Dilthey,[19] whose understanding of personality types she discusses, she expands his notion into a general epistemological notion.[20] As such it refers to a category into which the mind organises things because these things (e.g. communities,[21] roses,[22] and plants growing in a particular landscape[23]) have certain features in common. These features may be more or less superficial, such that what seems to be of one type for a superficial glance may, to the one looking beyond to the fundamental features in which superficial typicality is rooted, really be of another.

Because the type is an instrument of interpretation, it is clear why Stein would not want any individual reduced to it: it would be to mistake the real being of the individual for a set of specific features certain individuals have and share.[24] Also: the type envisaged by an interpretation may show

---

18   Sawicki: *Body, Text and Science*, pp. 139–43; Borden Sharkey: *Thine Own Self*, pp. 178–84.

19   PE, IV, 7 (b).

20   Aufbau, VIII, A, II.

21   PPE, I, II, § 4, d), ee).

22   FEB, III, § 6.

23   Aufbau, VIII, II.

24   I will quote the passage concerning Dilthey's understanding of types of persons in German, since the translation might be part of what has occasioned the problem of seeing how Stein uses the term as a general interpretative tool, applying not only to persons (p. 132): 'Dank der Korrelation von Werten, Werterleben und Schichten der Person lassen sich von einer universellen Wertekenntniss aus aller möglichen Typen von Personen *a priori* konstruieren, als deren Realisationen die empirischen Personen erscheinen. Anderseits bedeutet jedes einfühlende Erfassen einer Persönlichkeit Gewinnung eines solchen Typs. [In the note:] Mit der Typenhaftigkeit der personalen Struktur steht nicht im Wiederspruch, dass jedes Individuum und jedes

the interpretation itself as having greater or lesser depth. Whether I thus interpret a specific person as having the personality type of a shallow person or of a virtuoso reveals as much about my own personality as it does of the one whose personality I take to be shallow or virtuoso. The use of other types is also, and in the same way, characteristic of the interpretation, in that it reveals its depth. The type can have this function for us because the essences of things are what they are: it is our provisional knowledge of them that can be typical of us.

The relationship between species and type is discussed by Stein in relation to the theory of evolution.[25] Here she shows that the idea of a species that could change by mutation shows biological descent to be insufficient

---

seiner konkreten Erlebnisse ein schlechthin Einmaliges ist, weil der Gehalt mehrerer Bewusstseinsströme prinzipiell nicht gleich sein kann.'

What Stein here affirms is the correlation between the *a priori* value world and all possible personalities: Personalities are comprehensible as instantiations of value responses to different combinations of specific values. Since Stein does not affirm that values are limited in number, we do not have to envisage the possibility that one day we would run out of values, and therefore have to recycle personalities. But it is a fact that some personalities are alike in some respects because they respond to (some of) the same values. This is what gives rise to talk about personality *types*.

The translation of the first sentence of the passage (by Waltraut Stein) is, however, the following: 'Because of the correlation among values, the experiencing of value and the levels of the person, all possible types of persons can be established *a priori* from the standpoint of a universal recognition of worth.' It is possible that Borden Sharkey reads this to mean that all persons fit on a scale of values, exemplify a rung on a ladder, a level in a hierarchy of values, and thus are, by the fact that they respond to values, unequal in worth. That, however, is not what Stein says. 'Von einer universellen Werterkenntniss aus' might in fact be better translated as 'from the standpoint of an absolute knowledge of values', as indeed Sawicki rightly renders it in her critique (Sawicki: *Body Text and Science*, p. 140).

Stein does not affirm that we have this absolute knowledge of values, except that it is available to us *a priori*, much like mathematics is available to us, i.e. accessible to intuition but nevertheless requiring (significant) work on our part (which may indeed be more than we are able for). She does affirm that *from* this (ideal) standpoint it would be possible to see personalities as realising different values, not, however, that each personality type has a specific value in relation to this standpoint.

25   Aufbau, I, V, II, 1.

to define what is meant by 'species' in biology. What is in fact meant, she claims, is the type, which biology with its descriptions attempts to grasp, it is ultimately the *a priori* characteristics enabling us to identify the being by the senses with or without the help of instruments. It is thus the type that explains how we can distinguish mutations of the species in the first place as deviating types occurring in the same line of descent. For this reason, she implies, the type must be regarded as fundamental compared to the concept of a species relying on descent, although the type does not by itself explain why the biological species became and remain relatively stable.

Stein also distinguishes between social types and the inborn predispositions which are ultimately formative from within the person's self-constitution or unfolding of potential. She sees the inborn types as being those of the human, the gender, the specific and the individual, so that these types discovered in each individual are fundamental to the social types, which in turn reform what is already formed.[26] Thus the inborn human 'type', with its overlay of the social type, *does* play the role Borden Sharkey thinks the 'species form' should, without involving a concept of species that relies on actual descent, and thus in fact insuring the essential equality among human beings, which Borden Sharkey sees endangered.[27]

This type, however, does not impose itself in any causal way on our interpretation. Nor is it absolutely certain that the social type does not deform the inborn type. This is always a matter that needs our attention: whether we accurately identify what things are is the question science must ask itself again and again. But even more importantly: it does not happen automatically that we recognise ourselves as human beings *first and foremost*. It is something every person must accomplish freely by letting themselves be motivated by the value of being human. That is why there is a need to affirm human *dignity*, i.e. a need to affirm that it is the type of the human among all the types with which I can identify and with which

26   Aufbau, VIII, II, 4.
27   Sawicki op. cit. is, on the other hand, not correct in thinking that the *a priori* intelligibility of the type compromises Stein's phenomenology: it rather characterises it, since eidetic intuition forms part of the phenomenological method, as it is practiced also by Stein.

I can identify my others, that *should* be identified as the type of which we all are, first and foremost.

This point about the type clarified, we can proceed to unpack the intuition that we have of human dignity; that the human being is of fundamental value. This unpacking relies on the explication of logical implications present within our experience which are not necessarily directly experienced. This explains why we do not necessarily have the insight in an actual manner: although we usually do have it implicitly and intuitively. Like a mathematical proof, which proves something of which we might have an intuition, and in a sense simply explicates, maybe laboriously, what lies in the intuition in such a manner as to support it, so an explication of our intuition of human dignity, following implications implicit in our valuing, may also support our intuition:

The I at the centre of experience as I experience it, I cannot in fact regard as being less important (as having less value) than any other element in my experience, because it always accompanies this experience in the manner of being always there in it for reflection. On reflection, this experience would not be experienced, were it not for the I, who is the pole of this, my experience. I, in other words, cannot experience anything without the I, and must consequently value it as highly as, or as higher than, anything else I can experience, since it is indispensable to this experience. My person, being the subject of valuation as I experience it, I cannot as a consequence value any less than the I, as it is by means of it that I experience valuation in the first place.

The other I, whom I identify in empathy, and whose experience together with mine contribute to my experience of inter-subjective objectivity, I cannot value any less than I value inter-subjective objectivity, since this latter relies on it. In so far as I experience an I to be indispensable to its own experience, I also experience inter-subjective objectivity to rely on the indispensability of this perspective, which is different from mine. In this sense I must value the indispensability of the other I higher than inter-subjective objectivity, as it underlies it and founds it. Likewise with the other person, indispensable to the other's motivated constitution of the world, as this motivated constitution contributes to my experience of value as inter-subjectively accessible and objective.

I must value the type of the human being as highly as inter-subjective objectivity as it is the objective form according to which subjective perspectives are interchangeable. In this way the type of the human being is indispensable to recognisable experience in the same way as I am indispensable to experience. My body and the body of the other along with the psyche of us both must be as valuable as the type of the human being since it is these elements along with the I and the person that allow us to identify each other as of this type.

It thus turns out that all the elements we have identified as pertaining to being human in our constitutional analysis of the human being are at least as valuable to us as inter-subjective objectivity, and as that includes everything in the world, the human being must be more valuable to us than the whole world, given that it co-originates its constitution. It is for this reason that we feel the whole world disturbed by disregard for the human being: it turns the world upside down and institutes chaos in our perception of it. That human dignity should be respected means that the human being has importance for everything, that it has fundamental value, value that cannot be subordinated to any other value without it being wrong. As 'dignity' means a fundamental value, a value that is axiomatic and underlies other values, and which in turn is not founded on any other value, affirming human dignity means that we affirm that human beings have this fundamental value, and hence that we think this value should be placed higher than any other value, that it is indeed fundamental.

***

We have looked at Stein's value theory and her constitutional analysis of the human being and person. This we have done in order to assess how we constitute the value of the human person, i.e. how we come to think that the value of the human being is fundamental. It seems that we do come to constitute this value as fundamental because it is difficult for us to constitute ourselves as dissociated from the type of the human being and person, and that therefore the fundamental value which we must accord to the I as the means by which all our experience reaches us, must be extended not only to other Is but to all the elements that render the Is recognisable to each other as human Is. That it is difficult does not mean it is impossible. I can constitute myself on another type than the human type, but if I do that, my human experience disintegrates. Were I to constitute myself on the type of the 'animal', i.e. identify myself (primarily) as a animal, the world constituted as a result would not be objective, in the sense of being structured by knowable objects by which one may be knowingly motivated. Were I to constitute myself on the type of the 'woman' (only, as distinct from 'human being'), the experience of man would be in principle unintelligible, and therefore disturbing for my worldview, rendering it unstable and untenable.[28]

When we affirm human dignity, as is done in the preamble to most human rights instruments, we affirm that the value of the human being is highest among values, and that being human is more important than being for example man, white or of independent means. We affirm that among the possible types with which I can identify, the human one is of the highest value.

It makes sense that this implicit valuation underlies and explains the call to self respect and non-subservience identified by Stein as a call to autonomy. Once performed, it is certainly a good possessed by every human individual, and as such the ultimate foundation of justice, in the manner also perceived by Stein. But even if the valuation is not accomplished, the idea of human dignity would still be there ready to be affirmed, inspire self-respect, desired and serve as a foundation for justice. It is in fact unlikely we can reach any sense of justice, as is well understood also by the human rights tradition, without appeal to this notion. Hence the desire to understand what it involves.

---

28   See also Chapter 8.

CHAPTER 6

The Formation of Christian Europe

As Stein wrote her two volume philosophical and theological anthropology with the goal of providing a theoretical foundation for Catholic education (*Aufbau der menschlichen Person* and *Was ist der Mensch?*), she chose the following as the title of the first chapter: 'The idea of the human being as basis for the theory and practice of education'. For Stein ideas have essential (i.e. ideal, not real) being, which can be disclosed to spiritual beings.[1] But for human beings, who live as spiritual beings in space and time, such disclosure happens gradually in the world, in a process of education which initially is far more familiar to us than the idea it discloses, despite the latter being more intelligible in itself. Stein underwent such an educational process herself, like all human beings do, and her reflection on this process was the means by which she could clarify the idea of the human being needed for it. Education is not something one can dispense with, as it happens, and with great consequence for society, whether one pays specific attention to it or not. The most important thing that happens in education is in Stein's view the discovery of the image of the human being, in accordance with which one will accept to be formed oneself. This idea had in the final analysis to be Christian, she thought, as only the image of God can do justice to what the human being is meant to be.

In order to understand the connection between the education of individuals and the formation of communities, and show how this connection obtains in Europe, I would like to describe, as Stein does in various ways, the educational process, i.e. the process of becoming human (1).[2] Then I will explain the formation of communities happening in this process,

1   FEB, III.
2   See in particular Bildung, Aufbau, and Frau (Woman), but also Chapter 7.

according to Stein's early work *Philosophy of Psychology and the Humanities* (2). This accomplished, we should be equipped to understand the influence of Christianity on the European and on the formation of Europe as such (3). As these reflections are proposed freely after Stein, I will finally remind the reader of what I have taken from Stein, in order to make my own interpretation as transparent as possible.

The process of education

Waking up is a metaphor for beginning that we might use when attempting to understand the experience of the very small child. The presence of the other is necessary for the survival of the child, and thus empathy is available as the child awakes. Awakening, the child finds another experience with which it can itself empathise and in which it meets another, which is like itself.[3] Like chickens follow the first living thing they see, so the awakening spirit follows whatever appears to it as spiritual. A so fragile, open and vulnerable following like that of the child can only be experienced in deep connectedness. Such connectedness supposes, however, that the child is other compared to the one it faces. The German word for child – 'Kind' – seems to be etymologically related to the English word for species, 'kind', and also to the word we use for the attitude of kindness, to be 'kind'. At any rate, this similarity of words illustrates well that to be called a child means to be recognised as being of the same kind as those who call you child and also to be regarded as friendly. If the child is raised by living beings who are not human beings, then it learns no language: the *mimesis* characteristic of living beings by the means of which it learns, leaves it running about on all fours like a dog if it is raised by wolves, and learning a language if it is raised by human beings. The child thus forms itself according to the image it recognises as its own: the image of those it regards as being of its kind.

3   PE, III.

Thus the child learns to do and to think what those of its kind do and think. It learns what is possible within the inter-subjective space constituted by those it recognises to be of its kind. At first this space is the family, later it will be culture, religion and society, as it becomes understood how the family is connected with a larger community. These three dimensions of inter-subjective space are generated from generation to generation and manifest in traditions and institutions that structure the social world. The culture, in which the child is initiated and from which it learns, is led by visionaries, which have discovered and keep open various domains of the true. This function can be called 'prophetic', as its leaders often are pioneers and must convince others of the truth they have discovered; for example concerning hunting, gathering, agriculture, hygiene, childrearing, medicine, manners, trade, diplomacy, production and use of tools, technology, music, literature and all forms of knowledge, eventually establishing themselves as the various sciences. The possibilities that such prophets point to and keep open for others are possibilities to gain insight into truths that make the future foreseeable. In this way the pioneers of culture are like seers who look into the future by opening up knowledge of what things are and how they work.

Religion, led by priests and priestesses, offers a meeting with the supernatural or the whole, which perhaps has an influence on the world as we experience it, and which one therefore must know or recognise in order to have a complete understanding of the world. Kings and Queens in contrast lead into the socially possible and open up the state as the space of sovereignty by conquest, defence, expansion and the maintaining of power.

Thus the child learns truth from prophets and prophetesses, it learns the fear of God and the meaning of sin and justice from priests and priestesses, and from kings and queens it learns about limits and power. In this manner it is initiated into culture, religion and society. As a child it learns among other children, and thus also experiences what happens to other children when they transgress limits, commit sins or gain insight into some truth. It learns about the different possibilities for girls and boys, about the real and possible relations between prophetic, priestly and royal people, and comes to ask itself what it shall do when it grows up, which role it is to play in culture, religion and society.

The parents, like the leading persons accompanying the young growing up, accompany the child with a question that sometimes is suppressed by fear or egotism, but which nevertheless makes itself increasingly felt whether as enlivening or as destabilising for the relationship with the child: 'who are you?'. There comes a day when this question must be answered by the child. The necessity of the answer might lead to a crisis, whether because the child refuses to answer or because what it has to say is unacceptable. The continuation of the traditions in culture, religion and society depend on the answer: only the one who identifies him or herself as belonging to this culture, this religion, and this society will carry on the traditions and confirm the existence of the world of the parents and *maiores*, the inter-subjective space held open by them.

The child is in this manner surrounded by expectations. To take up responsibility means to meet these expectations. In the taking up of responsibility it is decided who the child is and with the implicit response to the question herewith given, the future identity of the parents and of the group is also decided. Often the child must explain its identity to the group: it must explain what it wants, what it takes to be true, and what it understands as sin and limits. Thus those called to prophecy always were made to do under some form of examination. Often priests and priestesses, as well as the governing, would also be called to explain in one form or another. Jesus did in particular, the one who the Christians recognise not only as Prophet, but also as High Priest, and King of Kings. He attempted with great care to answer the question concerning his identity, and his answers are still with us: 'Before Abraham was, I am'; 'my Father and I, we are one'; 'I am the resurrection and the life'; 'You say it, I am a king, but my kingdom is not of this world'.[4]

Not all children have something as astounding to say about their own identity. Yet, many children are a great surprise for their parents and elders in that their deepest understanding of the order of the world poses such a challenge, that the parents and elders may be shattered by it for years. Most parents and elders think deeply about the personal choices of their children

---

4   For example John, 8, 58; 11, 25; 18, 37.

and successors. They carry, like the mother of Jesus, 'all these things in their heart'. Only the most inhumane parent remains completely unconcerned by the destiny of their child. As soon as the 'I am ...' of the child is forthcoming, the parents and the elders begin to process the answer the child gives, including the hesitations it may have in giving the answer. They marvel at it, accept it and permit it, or they reject it, frown on it and prohibit it. This begins a new educational phase in the life of the parents and elders, in which they begin to discuss the meaning of true culture, right religion and the just society not only among themselves, but now also with their children. Perhaps a rupture occurs; perhaps institutions and traditions fall apart, or are developed and carried on in a new manner. Perhaps they remain the same. If the child is not killed or expelled in this crisis, it may proceed to become itself prophet, priest or king, and begin to compare its youthful courage to the recklessness of the 'new' young people. At this point the child has long been a parent itself, and a new awareness of finitude makes it reflect on the passing of things.

Many things become better, and much that was good falls into desuetude. In the meantime the child may have to take responsibility also for its parents. Now it will be tested whether the development of a respectful understanding between the generations has succeeded. Will the parents be able to recognise their own image in the child, the image according to which they will from now on be formed, the image the child has of them? When death comes, the wish to take leave from each other reconciled manifests itself. That often means, however, to allow oneself to understand the entire world, culture, religion and society, as relative to this one need of love, especially when there have been conflicts between child and parents. Then the accompaniment of a parent towards death can become a breakthrough in the educational process for both parties: in the open attitude of the person dying the one who accompanies him or her meets the questions concerning his or her own death and the goal of human life as such.

In this light the fact of belonging to the *maiores* is no longer so terrifying, even if the space they inhabit between power and ridiculousness, use and superfluousness, knowledge and insecurity to younger people often look uninhabitable. Here is the place of wisdom and help, and also the reflection on what true help is. Added is the experience of physical and psychological fragility, and then the dying itself, and with it the question of whether one has finished the task, and of what the task in fact was. Education now reaches its end. Whereto then? What for? For the last time the question of the meaning of life is raised and the experience of others who have died become the sounding board for one's own openness to what happens next.

The educational process of the individual is thus always accomplished in relation to others, as the image according to which I should be formed is presented by others as being my own. Education is therefore essentially connected to the formation of the community. We shall now turn to this formation in order to see how ideas, like that of Christianity, spread by being simultaneously community creating and educating for the individual.

The formation of community

The educational process of the individual essentially concerns the community. As soon as the child is there, there is, if the child is to survive, others of its kind who provide for it, and in whose world it attempts by imitation and empathy to penetrate.

In their world it encounters more others, and as it spends time in their company, it learns to identify specific roles, which structure the inter-subjective space. We have sketched this structure by distinguishing culture, religion and society. To the formation of community it is essential that the child is introduced and educated into already existing relationships so that it comes to know the possibilities that these provide. When the child chooses from among the possibilities presented to it what it wants to learn and who it is, it either contributes to the traditions, or to their transformation, or it separates itself from the community, perhaps to become part of another.

Values or motivational relationships handed on or protected by traditions can motivate in a threefold way.[5] Values can simply move us, so that we personally and freely with insight let ourselves be motivated. As values can motivate different persons, they allow for collaboration around the realisation of these values: this collaboration is the basic element in community. From this co-motivatedness one can distinguish two other motivational relationships, association and sentient contagion. I can decide to join a specific association without sharing the values the association stand for. I can in fact want to become a member for reasons other than the values of the organisation: in order to become influential, for example. Then I know I make a decision, which strengthens a certain tradition in principle, but which is made on the condition that this tradition allows me to realise other values I want to realise. Finally there is the possibility to let myself be contaminated with motivation through sentient contagion, i.e. through a kind of suggestion, which often is not conscious and is characteristic of the mass. Here I obtain energy to do something from what others do, like fish or birds know to follow each other in a school or a flock. In this way I can take over opinions and think what everyone else does, because everyone else thinks so. That happens mostly because I do not think about it, so that I do not realise what is happening, at least while it is happening.

When the child must determine its identity it can correspondingly draw from three sources: the spiritual world; the already existing organisations or associations in the world; and general opinion, the sum of expectations weighing on it. All three are ways of accessing spiritual energy, but in very different ways. As a result of how we go about accessing motivation, communities are formed in this process of personal identification. They are carried by the personal value response of human beings, sustained by associations and organisations in the world, and handed on by sentient contagion. In the final analysis the concrete community depends on the motivation of its members and is defined in its character by the distribution

---

5   This corresponds to the distinction made by Stein between community, association and mass, developed in PPH, II as constituted by the I.

of community carriers, organisation members or followers of available motivation.

In this way we are determined by our values, presented to us by culture, religion and society, and by the way we access the motivating power of these values. The 'we', which we in our valuing constitute as 'ours', allows us to create and legitimise institutions. We are dependent on this 'we' in so far as we want to accomplish something in the world, which relies on collaboration. This concerns in particular education, which reaches into all dimensions of inter-subjective space.

The limits of our communities occur where people belong to different cultures, religions or societies than the ones 'we' belong to. There, other laws than ours obtain, and thus one lives there at one's own risk, without the protection of our laws.

Communities live from the spiritual attitude of its members and also change according to it. New members, like children, must be educated to be able to take the attitude required for participating in the community. In this process they might also challenge and test anew the limits of the community. Thinking about this process can lead to the discovery of deeper, more universal laws, and to the consequent enlargement of the community. Then the previous 'we' is experienced as part of a more comprehensive 'we'.

It may also happen that new and foreign rules brought in by community members calls forth insecurity to such an extent that it leads to confrontations, maybe in the form of prohibitions, maybe in the form of violent clashes. All mass movements are characterised by their low threshold of tolerance: nationalism and religious or ideological fanaticism excludes the other, whose laws in principle cannot be recognised in so far as they cannot be reconciled with ours. Societies, which rely principally on such movements, are as a consequence usually totalitarian, and make use of instruments of ideological hygiene to keep the group coherent. Here personal identity must be experienced as relying entirely on the group, as the group needs to be regarded as an end in itself, instead of merely resulting from the process of identification, which education is. In order to secure identity and community, attempts at controlling these abound. But because community is the spiritual living together of human beings, which although conditioned through the management of society and the masses cannot be created or destroyed by these, such attempts at control ultimately leads only to a motivational deficit and loss of life. In the meantime these attempts at exerting control are for many deadly while they for others constitute a new possibility.

Therefore attempts at controlling culture, religion and society give rise to two opposed social tendencies in inter-subjective space. The first is a tendency towards conformity, which in the process tolerates suppression of the freedom of expression, religious freedom and the right to travel and settle where one wants. The second is a tendency towards pluralism and globalisation, which in the process tolerates the disintegration of national and religious identity of individuals and groups, traditions and institutions. In earlier times the freedom of expression was often subordinated to the interests of religion, and religious freedom was subordinated to the interests of the nation, in order to create a homogenous society it was possible to rule. In this way the European nation state arose at the expense of the shedding of much blood. At the same time the search for a deeper and more inclusive lawfulness counterbalanced the negative side of conformity. Thus there were always people who could see the human being in the Poles, the Jews and the Germans, whether they were Protestant, Catholic or Muslim. Such people, in virtue of their inclusive image of the human being constituted a new community with which the process of globalisation began, and which already had, *ipso facto*, committed itself to pluralism.

The influence of Christianity on the education of the European

Such a convinced universalist – the Jew Saul of Tarsus, the Christian and the Roman Citizen Paul – brought the news of Jesus Christ to Rome, in order to obtain from there the greatest possible public for the 'I am …' of a particular Jewish child, as he thought it concerned not only the Jews, but the whole of humanity. There were others who were deeply moved by Jesus' life and death and whom we are told went to Europe in order to announce the good news to the heathens: the three Marys, for example, who are celebrated by the Roma in Provence, and Peter, who is buried under St Peter in Rome.

The 'I am ...' of the adult Jesus, which had led to his crucifixion, was to these people and to those who listened to them, something very special, greater than anything they had hitherto encountered. They probably did not know what consequences it would all have, but they had to proclaim it. And what was one to do with such sayings as his? 'I am the way, the truth and the life'; 'cut off from me you can do nothing':[6] a child who so simply knows himself to be son of God that he offers his body as a sacrificial meal; proposes himself as reconciliation with God; and embodies the resurrection. What is one to think about that?

In awe, people decided to recognise Jesus as Prophet, High Priest and King of Kings –that was something they could do – and thus his unfathomable sayings, with the decisive events of his life, became part of the traditions of culture, religion and society. In the end these were so strongly marked by Christ that we still today, 2000 years later, speak of Christian culture, a Christian religion and of a secular state as distinguished from the Kingdom of Heaven proclaimed by Jesus.

Many other 'I am ...' have come and gone and have marked and reformed our traditions. There is no doubt, however, that these traditions drew and still draw significant strength – also for their power to create community – from the 'I am ...' of Christ and his followers, to the point where even kings and emperors would make use of them, in order to legitimise their authority. If Europe has come together in a particular way compared to other communities it goes back on the one hand to Constantine's decision to make Christianity the official religion of the Roman Empire, and on the other to the quest for power of tribal leaders at the borders of the Roman Empire, who could enter history as kings if they were baptised, and by this fact make their kingdoms recognised parts of the Christian – formerly

6   For example John 14, 6; 15, 5.

Roman – world.[7] One encounters the limits of Europe, in so far as one can speak of such, in those places where the authority of kings and of the state was never legitimised through Christianity: there Europe stops. With the establishment of the community of those who follow Christ, the idea also occurs, that the kingdom of God is not of this world, which means that a secular state is possible in this world, an idea that in fact became one of the most significant elements of the Christian and European heritage, whether handed on through culture, religion or society.

With it other ideas occurred, which characterise the European and the Christian tradition(s), in particular that it is possible, and indeed a fact, that the completely Other, God himself, meets us in every child. Thus it was with the One who was crucified, and who identified himself with all children as he said: 'whoever receives one of these little ones in my name, receives me'.[8] What we call European individualism surely has its roots in the idea of God's personal identification with every single individual.

If a child possibly brings with it the Transcendent into the world, it may also be that it knows better than the parents, and indeed than all the elders. Only when this is possible, can one get the thought that culture, religion and society can develop. Then traditions and institutions do not have to represent the eternal transcendent by their unchangeability. Then they are set free to find their end in the fulfilment of human beings. The European idea of progress was formed in this way: institutions and traditions can be improved on, because they can be better adapted to serve the needs of human beings.

Also the European idea of science has its roots here. Only the one who trusts that human beings may discover something by themselves believes that the human being, regardless of status, race, religion, gender or general opinion, has dignity and therefore is able to interpret traditions and institutions in such a way as to become aware of new truth. Without this confidence in human dignity, knowledge would be impossible, as power

7   For example Merovingians and Carolingians among the Franks, Harald Bluetooth in Denmark, Miezko in Poland and Rollo in Normandy.
8   For example Mk 9, 37.

and *raison d'etat*, which direct according to circumstances and interest, would attempt to produce knowledge in such a way that it perhaps would be useful in a certain sense and to some, but apart from this have no meaning. And who would then be left to say what 'useful' really means?

***

Stein's philosophy has contributed significantly to this analysis of the formation of Europe, as it provided the phenomenology of values, which made it possible to investigate the connection between personal value response and forms of community. Thus a phenomenology of inter-subjectivity has unfolded according to her example, allowing for analyses of culture, religion and society, in relation to the individual and its education into them. The sketchy division of inter-subjective space in culture, religion and society does not stem from Stein, but is compatible with her thought. By means of this sketch, we obtained the possibility to continue the analysis of traditions and institutions begun by Stein, in such a manner as to clarify the influence of Christianity on the formation of inter-subjective space we call 'Europe'.

PART II

Metaphysics

CHAPTER 7

Education of the Human Person

Every work reflects the one who wrought it, the time it was forged in, and the purpose for which it was conceived. That is why Stein's *The Structure of the Human Person* is a key not only to Stein's entire work, but also to the Jewish experience in Germany in the nineteen thirties, and to the philosophy of education as such. It reveals Stein's deep commitment to the human person, constitutes her *Auseinandersetzung* with National Socialism, and argues for the centrality of the human being in education theory. In the following discussion these three aspects will be examined. First we will look at Stein's education theory in the context of her entire work, assessing the influence that education had on the elaboration of her philosophy and her understanding of the philosophical significance of education (1). Next we will deal with the work as part of history: its precedents and antecedents, what occasioned it and what it, in turn, occasioned. Its sources constitute a significant part of its precedents, and the method a significant part of what it handed on. Hence these are examined as aspects of the work's history (2). Finally, the structure of the work is exhibited, beginning with Stein's justification for understanding the theory of education as philosophical and theological anthropology and ending with her account of the constitution of the human person in its essential openness (3).

'*Aufbau*' (as in the work's German title: *Der Aufbau der menschlichen Person*), means structure, construction and edification. The literal sense of 'edification' – the building of an edifice – gives us the active sense of the German word, whereas 'structure' gives us the passive sense. Education, in German, is *Bildung*; close in meaning to the English 'building', and, like it, having the same double sense, active and passive: the activity of building, and the finished building resulting from the activity.[1] The human person, therefore, for Stein, is built and builds itself up according to a structure it has, or gets as it builds. As education literally shapes who we are, the structure of the human person is the central question of education theory.

Stein's theory of education

When Stein composed *The Structure of the Human Person* in 1932 at the age of forty, she had spent nine years teaching German and Latin with the Dominican nuns in Speyer. A lecturing career in philosophy had been denied her, but she had tutored for Husserl as well as privately in Breslau after she graduated in 1917 until she accepted the job as a secondary school teacher. Teaching was part of how Stein envisaged herself: She was a teacher.[2]

Her earliest phenomenological works provide the foundation for her later theory of education. They do not explicitly touch on the topic, but explore the fundamental structure of the inter-subjectively constituted human person. Education, which so decisively contributes to this constitution, is implicitly given a central place awaiting development. Like any communicative practice, education projects an understanding of shared humanity, which it poses implicitly as goal and standard for communication. This standard – the structure of the human person, who is communicative and stands in relation to others, whom it recognises as being like itself – is brought out (*e-ducere, ausbilden*) or built up (*edify, aufbauen*) in education.

The inter-subjective setting is explored in *On the Problem of Empathy*, where it is shown how the act of empathy contributes to the constitution

---

1   'Zur Idee der Bildung' in Bildung I, 4, pp. 35–49.
2   The best account of Stein's life, apart from her own – *Life in a Jewish Family* – is Waltraud Herbstrith, *Edith Stein. A Biography*, transl. by Fr. Bernhard Bonowitz, O.C.S.O (San Francisco: Ignatius Press, 1992).

of the human person (constituted simultaneously in the self and in the other through recognition). The physical, bodily, psychic and spiritual aspects are all examined as dimensions that the I must attribute to itself (and attribute to the self of the other) in order to make sense of experience. Education, it can be seen on this background, works consciously with the self-identification of the human person in and through its relations with things and persons.

The two treatises making up *Philosophy of Psychology and the Humanities* investigate the limits of the human person (once again, as they are experienced, i.e. as they are constituted). The first investigates the limits regarding nature (constituted as obeying the law of causality), and the second investigates the limits regarding the spirit (constituted by obeying the laws of motivation). The human person is experienced as both caused (in the state of tiredness, for example) and motivated (by values): The person becomes familiar with its individuality through its body and through the communities of which it forms part. Energy (*Kraft*) straddles the spheres of nature and spirit, and it is experienced as a property of the psyche which can be spent and loaded up again, precisely by drawing energy from these two realms – nature and spirit. It is above all this phenomenon that makes the I constitute itself as a person existing in relation to both nature and spirit. Energy manifests the individuality of the person, an individuality that is constantly challenged by natural forces from without and spiritual forces from within. Helping the individual to meet these challenges and bring his or her individuality to full bloom is thus assisting in the process of self-identification, the process of the 'construction' or '*Aufbau*' of the human person.

In the second part of *Philosophy of Psychology and the Humanities*, *Individual and Community*, Stein also investigates how valuation is community-forming. Whereas valuing the same values is not the only way in which community is formed, it is nevertheless the most important way. Values are spiritual motivating factors, and when they are shared, they bring people together. It is by a person's own self-constitution (self-identification), that the values preferred by this person make him share a world with others, who also constitute themselves in a like manner. Values, thus, make people share the same 'structure'; the same 'construction'; the same '*Aufbau*'. There is a hierarchy among these values – they are all preferred by some, but not everyone takes everyone into account. The superficial person takes into account only those values which to others would appear minor: e.g. the values of pleasure and comfort. The less superficial person takes into account also the values that go beyond these, say courage and knowledge. But the depths are searched only by those who value the highest values, such as the holy, the true, the good and the beautiful.[3] Hence the depth of the persons directly reflects the depth of the spiritual community they share. But sharing values and forming community is not the only way to live together. Association relies on agreement (not immediately on value response), and the forming of the masses relies on sheer physical and psychic togetherness. These more superficial forms of sociality are not less important for all that. They, in fact, constitute the 'buffer-zones' in which not sharing the same values, and yet maintaining some sort of order, is possible. However, they are essentially fragile and reflect the surface orientation of the individuals affected by them. Education can and must open up the person to his or her own depths, as well as to the deeper values of the community, because the cohesion of society, its basis in community, depends on that.

An Investigation Concerning the State, finally, compares the different kinds of sociality in and through which the person is constituted and examines, in particular, the state's making, validation and confirmation of Law. The constitution of the state, and of the person as a citizen, seems in practice to rely on community, but in principle it relies on a significant development of associational structures. Hence the state is fragile to the extent that its basis is, i.e. it may disintegrate if the community supporting it disintegrates.[4] Stein examines and explains the tension between nation

3   Stein's value- and community theory owes much to Scheler. See in particular his *Formalism in Ethics and Non-Formal Ethics of Values*. Here we have made use of a Schelerian distinction between the values of the hedonist, the hero, the genius and the saint to exemplify the idea that depth of soul corresponds to height of value. However, Stein does not explicitly refer to this schematisation of the objective value hierarchy.

4   Jürgen Habermas, 'The European Nation-State: On the Past and Future of Sovereignty and Citizenship', in *The Inclusion of the Other*. Habermas shares Stein's insight that

(*Volk*) and state (*Staat*), as a tension inherent in the personal identity of each and every person contributing to the life of the community and/or of the state. Political dramas are therefore also personal ones, and we are led back to the role of the educator: only the awakening of the depths of the person can prevent superficiality and its blind exclusion of the other, and only anthropology can teach us about these depths.

These early phenomenological works, however, are not alone in underlying Stein's education theory in *Der Aufbau der menschlichen Person*. A second phase of Stein's philosophical development plays a major role in relation to the manner in which her insights matured. When Stein received baptism in 1922, she started seeking a deeper understanding of the Catholic tradition, and was advised to study Thomas Aquinas. Accepting this suggestion, she decided to translate *De veritate* into German, and to comment on it.[5] Question XI is dedicated to 'the teacher', and Stein understands it to concern the genesis of knowledge, much like constitution does.[6] She

---

nation and state each obey a different logic, and that the state relies on the nation to be what we have come to take for granted that it is. Today the problems faced by the Nation State are those of immigration and globalisation. The problem Stein observed taking shape was that of the allergy of the German nation towards its internal other: the Jews, who themselves constituted a nation – somewhat despite themselves.

5   Stein wanted to make accessible the thought of Thomas Aquinas to her contemporaries. This made her recast his questions in treatise form, thinking the objections and their answers into the body of the text. Such reconstruction gave her plenty of scope for rethinking Aquinas' thought and informing her own. The result is a translation and commentary all in one.

6   She sums it up in the following manner: 'We are here given a brief sketch of the *genesis* of knowledge. God gives us the "light" of reason, i.e. the formal power to know, and also with it certain contents, from which all knowledge – by acquisition of further material by means of the senses – is to be derived. In principle the human being does not need another teacher. It is possible that he, on the grounds of his natural gifts and through the work of reason, progresses and expands his knowledge to the point of full capacity *in via inventionis*. But a threefold support by created teachers is possible. He could be shown truths of a spiritual nature by means of sensible signs, truths deducible from principles and in this process of deduction actualising potential knowledge (in what way is not further stated). He could be stimulated by being provided with images to work as material for the reasoning activity, and he

found in Aquinas someone who understood the human being to be freely training him- or herself in virtue, and this allowed her to integrate his insights with her own phenomenology, much like Aquinas had assimilated Aristotle from his Christian standpoint. *The Structure of the Human Person* together with its theological counterpart *What is the Human Being?* testify to this integration of the old with the new. The old was, on the one hand, the Scholastic tradition that had provided vocabulary, method and material for the new phenomenology. But on the other hand 'the old' was this same phenomenology, which had made the first sharp imprint on Stein's mind, now making room for the 'new' *philosophia perennis*.

History in *The Structure of the Human Person*

The two volumes of education theory were conceived as two parts of a course Stein was to teach at the Marianum at Münster, the teacher-training College where she had found employment after giving up her teaching engagements in Speyer. But due to the Nazi prohibition on Jewish professionals she did not teach the second half: *What is the Human Being?* The theological part of the foundation for the theory of education she had planned was thus never given as a series of lectures, but was instead written up as a treatise.

Her newly gained lack of employment opened up for her the way into the Cologne Carmel. Her last major works: *Finite and Eternal Being* and *Science of the Cross* were conceived and brought to fruition in Carmel. They continued to deepen her understanding of the human person and to develop, in particular, the value of its individuality. Here she graduated

---

could have the formal power of reason strengthened. The first kind [of teaching] is open to humans and angels, but the second and third kinds only to angels (in what way remains in the dark)'. DV, pp. 324–5.

to write for 'beginners' as a 'beginner'[7] and to conceive herself more and more as one of many, one among many, searching for the meaning of being.

From her earliest youth Stein had been interested in the dynamics of community. She saw this as the key for understanding inter-subjectivity, and therefore for the understanding of what it was for anything to *be* – given that it was inter-subjectively constituted. The difficult social development of Germany after the First World War gave her the opportunity to test her sociological insights, and also forced her to consider her own identity. The Nazis shared this interest in the social: They were socialists – convinced of the importance of the collective identity for the individual: 'The People' was their idol. But they were not only socialists, they were *National* Socialists – wanting to establish a socialist state for the *Nation*, the *German* Nation – which, as it turned out, could not recognise any limits in relation to other peoples or nations. Stein recognised 'the People' to be of great importance. Her people, however, were those who 'belonged to her', 'those who had been given to her' – phrases she often used in her letters reflecting, in fact, phrases used by Jesus. She belonged to the human race. Stein's understanding of the ontological relationship between the person and his or her people is rooted in her value theory, which again is rooted in her understanding of self-identification as something essentially mediated by others.

The Structure of the Human Person records her awareness of 'the possibility of a meaningful and valuable human community life outside that of the nation' and 'the absolute measure of the value of peoples and persons'.[8] It is to this meaning of the individual, even when isolated from his community, that education must minister. Education has a direct social impact because it addresses the person him- or herself. The education Stein founds is one that recognises the importance of the nation, but also its relativity to the individual human person and to humanity as such.

She undertook this foundation in relation to the trends of times she lived in. These trends constitute, together with the Phenomenological and

---

7   FEB, preface of the author, p. xxvii.
8   Aufbau, VIII, III, 3., c) and f).

Scholastic traditions, the sources of her work. *German Idealism*, Heidegger's *Existential Philosophy* and *Psychoanalysis* formed, together with Darwin and contemporary notions in physics,[9] animal psychology,[10] anthropology,[11] sociology[12] and theology,[13] the background against which she formed her personal synthesis of Husserlian and Thomistic elements, and from which she criticised them. It had fallen into place through dialogue with various contemporary authors, mostly people she knew personally from the Göttingen Circle. First of these were Max Scheler, who had provided her with materials for her value- and community theory. But there was also, and in particular, Hedwig Conrad-Martius, her life-long friend and interlocutor in all matters ontological, and Dietrich von Hildebrandt, who (even though no personal acquaintance grew up between them) was referred to in

9   Her sources for this understanding are not clear.

10 E.g. Max Etlinger, *Beiträge zur Lehre von der Tierseele und ihrer Entwicklung* (Münster: Aschendorf, 1925).

11 E.g. Albert Huth, *Pädagogische Anthropologie* (Leipzig: Klinckhardt, 1932), referred to by Stein as exclusively based on natural science and omitting the spiritual dimension of the human being. Groethungsen: *Philosophische Anthropologie*, in Oldenburg: *Handbuch der Philosophie*, Abteilung III (Mensch und Character), 1931, is referred to by Stein as neglecting the systematic character of anthropology and replacing it with a historical exposition.

12 She recognises her debt to F. Tönnies as the distinction between *Gesellshaft* and *Gemeinshaft* elaborated by him continued to play an important role for her. Cfr. *Gemeinschaft und Gesellschaft: Grundbegriffe der reinen Soziologie* (1887). Transl. as: *Community and Society*, by Charles P. Loomis (New York: Harper and Row, 1963).

13 The Bible is referred to a number of times, especially to exemplify the formation of the State of Israel out of the community of a wandering tribe as pictured in the Old Testament. Augustine is referred to when she defines the Catholic idea of education. Most often, however, Christian doctrine is referred to as such. It is understood as a living body of thought ('truths') based on the revelation of God. An example of such a truth is 'the human being is created by God'. Another example is 'every single human soul is created by God'. She also refers to a specific idea of Christian, and in particular of Catholic, education (I. A. II. 2. b). The second volume of her education theory is a commented tapestry of statements from Denziger-Bannwarts, *Enchiridion Symbolorum, definitionum et declarationum de rebus fidei et morum*, in the edition of 1928.

relation to ethics. Her synthesis equipped her with a 'method' she insisted was phenomenological: 'Developed by Husserl in the second volume of his *Logical Investigations*', this method is 'in my opinion used by all great philosophers of all times even if not exclusively and with clear reflective understanding.'[14] 'The most elementary of principles in phenomenology [... is ...] to fix on the things themselves. Not to engage in theories [...] but to approach things, without prejudice, in immediate intuition [...] The second principle is: to pay attention to what is *essential*.' Taking Aquinas as a guide in the choice of problems did not mean adopting his 'system', even less expounding his anthropology.[15] The method that Stein handed on was, therefore, one that took into account the necessity for a starting point insisted on by Descartes. It revisited the problems of the philosophical tradition before him to find in it insights that could be reached from this starting-point and to discard others that could not. Finally, it criticised elements of the tradition after Descartes in the same manner, accepting the elements of Enlightenment, Darwinism, Psychoanalysis and Existentialism that could be reached from the starting-point while discarding those that could not. What she handed on, was thus a method that could integrate whatever was found to be of value in any tradition.[16]

14   Aufbau, II, II, 2.
15   Such a task would be 'a great and beautiful one, but would complicate mine, as I cannot simply follow the teaching of St Thomas, but differ in understanding on several important points.' Aufbau, II, II, 1. These points concern in particular Thomas' understanding of matter as the principle of individuation and the consequent lack of understanding of personal individuality, and of experience as being valuable as such. It is quite likely that anthropological notions based on St Thomas were, implicitly or explicitly, part of Stein's brief for founding Catholic education theory. At any rate, Aquinas' value as a *topos* in this regard would have been considerable at the time. It is her experiential starting-point that prevents Stein from simply accepting Thomas' anthropological ontology and leads her to rethink his problems by the means of the new method.
16   'Method' could here be put in quotation marks to acknowledge Gadamer's hermeneutical insight that truth and method cannot be separated. Cfr. H.G. Gadamer, *Truth and Method*, trans. ed. by Garrett Barden and John Cumming (London: Sheed and Ward, 1975).

When Stein fled from Germany in 1938 to the Carmelite Convent of Echt in Holland, she brought with her several manuscripts, including *The Structure of the Human Person* and *What is the Human Being?*. These were placed in a backpack by her sisters in religion and hidden in the cellar of the friendly convent of Herkenbosch, thought to be a safe hiding place. In one of the last German air raids in 1944 the convent was completely ruined. The partly loose, partly bound, sheets of Edith Stein's manuscripts were rescued from the ruins and brought by Pater Avertanus, the Belgian provincial of the Carmelites, and Pater Herman van Breda OFM, the later Director of the Husserl Archives, to Louvain, where they were entrusted to Dr Lucy Gelber for reconstruction.[17] A meticulous reconstruction began, which bore fruit in terms of publication only as late as 1994. The public *Wirkungsgeschichte* of the work began thus only then.

The Structure of the Human Person

The Structure of the Human Person is divided into nine chapters, three of which are concerned with identifying the problem, establishing the method and delimiting the subject (the first two and the last). The remaining six chapters build the philosophical anthropology Stein proposes as a foundation for Catholic education theory.

Chapter I, 'The Idea of the Human Being as Foundation for Education as Science and Practice', argues that education is a practice relying in principle on an idea of the goals of education. 'Behind all human action stands a *Logos*, which guides it'.[18] This *Logos* explains the action and enables the actor to proceed meaningfully. 'All education concerned with forming

---

17 Lucy Gelber, 'Einleitung' in Aufbau (ESW XVI), p. 20. Lucy Gelber was at that time the archivist of the Husserl Archives. Her account of the painstaking reconstruction of the text is to be found the same place.

18 Aufbau, I, A.

human beings is led by a certain understanding of these, of their status in the world and their tasks in life, as well as by the practical possibilities of treating and forming them. The theory of human formation, which we call education theory, belongs organically within an entire worldview, i.e. in a metaphysics, and the idea of the human being is part of this worldview by which it is immediately concerned.'[19] Even if such a metaphysics is not explicit or even conscious, and even if a professed worldview does not always have an impact on practice in the way that it purports to, it is still at work, however obscurely, in practical education. Few people, especially teachers, would contest that education centrally concerns the formation of human beings. However, some politicians and administrators might view education in other terms, say, in terms of its socio-economic impact on the competitiveness of society, or as a means to realise certain political objectives. In such an understanding of education there also is an implicit worldview, namely that of education being a means to an end, where the latter may or may not differ from the human person itself. As Stein concentrates on the structure of the human person for founding education theory, she implicitly affirms that education centrally concerns the formation of human beings for their own sake as education is how they become who they are. Thereby the idea is also rejected that education should be a form of social engineering essentially unconcerned with the life and nature of the individual persons being educated. Education is, according to Stein, about the human person. Therefore she investigates three different ideas of being human (German Idealism, Depth Psychology and Existentialism), all of which influence the contemporary vision of the human being, and thus have an impact on contemporary education. In German Idealism 'the human being [...] is free, called to perfection (to "humanity"), a link in the chain of the entire human race, progressing towards perfection, providing every single one and every single people, because of their individuality, with a specific task in the development of humanity.'[20] On the

---

19   Ibid. The ambiguity is deliberate: the human being is immediately concerned by the
      worldview that includes a view of itself.
20   *Aufbau*, I, A, I, 1.

other hand confidence in the goodness of human nature and in reason, is unrealistic: It does not sufficiently take feelings and drives into account. Even if Romanticism did address this aspect, it did not break through to rectify the Idealist bias. It did, however, become a precursor of Depth Psychology, for the development of which Russian novels also played a role. The First World War and the confusion surrounding it ensured that rationalist idealism was definitively conditioned by various alternative images of the human being, but the unity and meaningfulness of the soul became a casualty of the act of dethroning rationality. As a consequence of the inability to identify a significant core of the human being, education was no longer meaningful. Positively, this tendency initiated a greater awareness and appreciation of the urges and drives of the human being, but negatively it had the effect that psychoanalytic explanation replaced mutual understanding, thus distorting the trust that must exist between human beings for education to begin and to succeed. Existentialism, thirdly, operates in the depths, like psychoanalysis, but it does not consider the human being capable of enduring for any length of time the questions raised by its own being. The flight into anguish, when not preoccupied with this or that particular thing, seems to be the most authentic approach the existential I can make to itself. Thus education becomes the senseless task of destroying the various ideals in which the soul takes refuge, in order for the soul to be delivered from its own non-being.

Beyond these three visions of the human being Christian metaphysics provides an alternative vision, expressing itself directly in education theory. It has a number of elements in common with the trends described. It shares with German Idealism the conviction of the goodness of human nature, but its reason for doing so is the belief that the latter is created by God in his own image. Human nature is spiritual in that it loves and knows, and hence is directed towards a commensurate goal of perfection beyond earthly existence. Thus Christian education shares with depth psychology the understanding that life without depth, i.e. without roots in what is not immediately accessible to reason, is a life misspent. Christian education reckons with the dark sides of human nature, so much that it considers it a task beyond the resources of the human being to find by itself the way out of their power. But through participation in Christ's filial relationship with

God the human being is enabled to play a role in Christ's mystical body and so to have a source of divine life in his or her own self, strengthening, healing and enlightening both will and intelligence for deeds beyond their own intrinsic power. The individual is responsible for not extinguishing this life of grace, to which end the thought of the reward of a life in glory greatly helps. Finally, the call to authentic being, as glimpsed in Heidegger's philosophy, is explained in Christian metaphysics as the movement from fragmentary being to wholeness in Christ. It forcefully expresses the call to inwardness away from the inauthenticity of the ways of the world.[21]

> To sum up we can say: seen from the point of view of Christian anthropology the humanistic ideal is revealed as reflecting the integrity of the human being before the fall, but its origin and its goal is left out of consideration, and the fact of original sin ignored. The vision of depth psychology is that of fallen man, even if conceived in a static and a-historic manner: past and future possibilities, as well as the fact of salvation, go unheeded. Existential philosophy shows us human beings in their finitude and essential nothingness. It concentrates on what the human being is not and is thus disconnected from what he is positively, as well as from the Absolute, which is figured behind the conditioned.[22]

The Christian educator must understand him- or herself merely as a helper, or an instrument, of the educator that God is. God alone knows what serves the individual best, and also what he or she needs to learn. The human educator can co-operate with God by adjusting herself or himself to the laws of the human being and to this particular human being in his or her care. Education theory serves this end, as do other sciences like psychology, anthropology and sociology; but the educational process itself must happen face to face as its medium is mutual openness. When closure has occurred, which for instance happens through hurt, then a turning back towards openness, which requires waiting, patience, creativity and faithfulness, must be initiated.[23] What education realises, therefore, is nothing

---

21   By, for example, Augustine in *Confessions* and *City of God*.
22   Aufbau, I, 1.
23   'Over-activity and passivity are equally great dangers in education. The road between these two pitfalls is the one that the educator must move along, and he is responsible

extrinsic to the human being. It is reciprocal communication of grace for the realisation of the common destiny in the unity of the eternal *Logos*. 'When the ideas of the human being are oriented towards it, then they constitute sufficient foundation for the science and practice of education.'[24]

Chapter II, 'Anthropology as Foundation for Education', sets out to further investigate the kind of anthropology that must underlie education theory. Anthropology inspired by natural science is useful in order to know the functions and developmental laws of the human body and to discern among these which are conducive to natural, harmonious development and which may produce harm. Scientific knowledge of different races may also be useful, in so far as individuals exemplify these, and the knowledge of them may further understanding of the individuals.[25] However, natural science is only conducive towards a useful educational anthropology in so far as the openness between subjects remains undisturbed. Scientific explanation cannot replace mutual understanding; if it does, education is denatured and the pupil has reason to close him- or herself off against the teaching proposed. As natural science possesses no normative standard according to which humanity, individual and race can be brought into unison, it can only serve as a means to establish the anthropology sought for.

The humanities may help us towards understanding the individual. They serve as a 'school of understanding', but they only touch upon the efficiency of spiritual power, which is of crucial importance to the educator. The humanities provide *anthropographics*, and hence are anthropology in the same sense as description of animals is zoology. But a general anthropology, which is the science of the human being as spiritual person, is part of a general philosophy of the spiritual, which includes community,

---

to God that he strays neither to the right nor to the left. Moreover, he can only move forwards while carefully probing. What must strengthen him in this terrible task is the thought of what makes the task so dangerous: that of God's work with which he must co-operate.' Aufbau, I, 2.

24   Ibid.

25   'The individual is not isolated, but is a member of supra-personal formations such as a people and a race, and the task of the educator is to form him, not only as individual, but as a member of the whole.' Aufbau, II, 1.

state, language, law and culture in general. Even if the humanities provide material for this, they provide no standard according to which discernment can be made of the importance in education of the supra-individual formations such as state, race and humanity. The educator must know, in his dealings with the spirit of the times, whether there is an objective order into which these fit. This standard must come from ethics, the philosophical discipline dealing with values. It is part of ontology, which makes use of the other sciences according to its purpose. But this is not all: 'A general ontology cannot limit itself to created being, but must take uncreated being into consideration as well as the relationship between these. Likewise, anthropology would be incomplete and insufficient as a foundation for education if it did not consider the relationship between human beings and God.'[26] Hence philosophical anthropology is essentially unfinished and can only be finalised by a theological complement. To approach this essentially open human person historical methods are available, but they are at once labour-intensive and inconclusive. Stein therefore does not pursue them. Systematic phenomenology is a more direct approach which must be employed instead, as it allows us to advance towards conclusions.

Chapter III begins the construction of the anthropology proper, as it treats of 'The Human Being as Material Thing and as Organism'. As we meet the human being, in ourselves and in others, it is a material thing, but it is also alive in soul and spirit. It reflects all levels of being, both the material and the spiritual, as a microcosm. As a material thing, natural laws apply to it. It has symmetry in common with other living beings of a higher order, and likewise spontaneous movement. The materiality of the body ensures acoustic givenness: The material thing that the human being is, not only 'sounds' when struck from the outside, but 'sounds' first and foremost on its own initiative by speech, in the same way as it moves itself first and foremost on its own initiative.

Chapter IV, 'The Human Being as Animal', investigates how the human being shapes itself by its own initiative, internally, into a shape called by Aristotle 'life-soul' (psyche). This life-soul makes the organism, from its

26 Aufbau, II, 4.

material, into a living being that moves. The power that the soul exercises over the body expresses itself in sensitivity and free movement, and its spirituality opens it towards both the outside and the inside. "'Having a soul" means having a centre in which all sensing of the outer world computes and from which everything appearing in bodily attitude as coming from within is brought forth.'[27] As in plants, the soul in humans searches upwards for light. As in animals, it responds to drives or instincts, in a manner, however, less secure than they.[28] The characteristics displaying themselves in the build of the body and in the character of the soul of animals are those of the species.[29] The importance of the individual in humans is accompanied by changes in their animal nature: the register of sounds is expanded into a language, for example, and the potencies of the soul require, because of their unlimited nature, a choice for any of them to be developed. The human species has specific characteristics, and all human persons are of this species: There is, however, no species of human persons – they are all individuals.

Chapter IV concerns 'The Problem of the Origin of Species' and the relationship between 'genus, species and individual'. The level of complexity observable in the different species suggests the possibility of order. This gives rise to the question of whether this order can be conceived of as an order of descent, or 'whether the species could be thought to have come from one another, and ultimately from one original form.'[30] 'Herewith the ground of description of facts is left behind; an explanatory hypothesis is proposed which must be supported either by general laws or by experiment

27   Ibid., IV, 2.
28   Stein does not admit of the two distinct levels of soul of the Aristotelian tradition, the vegetative and the animal; to her, rather, living beings are either plants or animals.
29   'There seems to be no individuality there, which as such would have meaning'. However, 'only a deeper analysis could convincingly establish that this marks an essential difference between animal and human: that in humans individuality gets a new sense, which cannot be found in any subhuman creature.' Aufbau, IV, 3. In FEB, Stein seems inclined to see individuality to be of consequence also in animals.
30   Aufbau, V, II, 1.

and observation.'[31] The first possibility of support by general laws is beyond experimental science, and the second possibility of support by experiment can only yield species that seem to constitute an 'in between' with regard to other species. That the hypothesis of Darwinian Theory remains a hypothesis does not preclude it from being correct; but whatever its status, the notion of species needs clarification. 'So far it has been used in a double sense: as an inner form shaping the animal and as the sum of all individuals which exemplify this form.'[32] When biologists speak of the 'origin' of species, they seem to imply a change of the form, or an origin of the form. The form, however, is what makes the individual as well as the species identifiable as the same throughout its development. In the most primitive forms of reproduction, i.e. cloning, the individual reproduced differs from its parents only in respect of external factors. If, therefore, a-sexual reproduction could give rise to new species, external factors such as the environment must be able to have an effect on the essence of the individual, to change its descendants into a new type of individual. 'If the creation of new individuals may be derived from a new creative impulse, then it is possible to think that the forms originated in procreation are also carriers of a "new" form; no necessity persists according to which this qualification should be sought in the procreating individuals. Only when one thinks one can, and must, derive every new form from the old alone, must one ask for the causes of the changes in the procreating individual.' Sexual reproduction gives great scope for variation as the gametes of two procreating individuals interact, and thus the formation of new species from old ones is 'essentially possible, but not necessary.'[33] 'It is possible that the plurality of forms relies on a plurality of independent principles. It is also thinkable, however, that there exists a principle regulating the entire domain, in which one transition from part-form to part-form took place within a great developmental order.'[34] 'Such laws would belong to the factual

---

31   Ibid.
32   Ibid.
33   Aufbau V, II, 8.
34   Ibid.

order of the created world; they would dictate the possibilities existing in principle which make a world constituted like ours real or thinkable.'[35]

Chapter VI addresses 'The Animal in Humans and the Specifically Human', and hence what exceeds the species in the person. According to the manner in which humans realise their potential, choice and responsibility is added in contrast with animals. We regard people as being responsible for what has become of them as the human being 'can and must form himself'[36] because he is an 'I', i.e. a spiritual pole, characterised by consciousness, openness and freedom. By this 'I' he *can* realise himself, and from this '*can* arises the possibility of the *ought*'.[37] The 'I' must form the *self*, i.e. the entire animal nature belonging to it as well as intentionality and freedom. To this conscious formation and responsibility there is no parallel in the subhuman animal kingdom. It is the person who, as an I, has a 'spiritual sense, which is only accessible in its own awareness of itself'.[38] This I, the person, has a body and a soul, and these are the self that it is responsible for. It carries this responsibility by searching for, finding, and not losing itself, i.e. by reaching the level of depth of soul sufficient for the understanding of its own self and its tasks. It thus must 'take itself in hand', experience the *ought*, and look around for others of whom it might think: such an 'I' should I be.

In Chapter VII, 'Soul as Form and Spirit', Stein criticises Thomas' doctrine of the unity of substantial form. She thinks that the 'personal-spiritual soul *largely* determines the form of the body, but not alone'.[39] The soul's openness to the spiritual world makes its separability from the body intelligible as the spiritual soul, 'the dominant form, which decides the

---

35   'But even if it was entirely believed, as only a neutral law can be, a materialistic and monistic worldview would not follow as a superficial popular philosophy would have it, nor would the Biblical creation narrative have been proved wrong.' Ibid. For Stein's understanding of how a comparison of Darwin's and Aquinas' concept of species might help us to clarify both, see Chapter 5.

36   Aufbau, VI, II, 1.

37   Ibid.

38   Aufbau, VI, II, 2.

39   Ibid., VII, I, 2.

telos, is one and can be seen as the authentically substantial one even if the concrete substance is not determined exclusively through it.'[40] What the entirety has in common is energy, a force that can be replenished from the material world, from others and from values. But even the energy is marked by the source from which it comes, and the soul's access to its depth is required for it to interpret and integrate its energies, and for the will to unite. The will, then, can receive powerful support from the will of God.

Chapter VIII, 'The Social Being of the Person', addresses the last and very important aspect of the human being. The point of view on the human being we have adopted so far is in fact an abstraction: the human person is not an isolated individual, but is determined by its social acts, functions and relationships. 'Communities grow spontaneously, either from shared life conditions and life in common (school class, village), from genetic descent (family, tribe, people), or – under the influence of free acts – by reason of personal reciprocal positioning and mentality (friendship, marriage), or because of common acceptance of a domain of values (scientific or artistic interest groups, community of believers). Mostly more, sometimes all, of these community-forming factors are in play at once.'[41] From such belonging to various communities the individuals come to be of various types (Irish, father of a family, middle class). A people is distinct from the individuals constituting it in that its experience as such is distinct from the experience of the individuals constituting it. Whereas a person is deeply in debt to his people, whose language and culture he has assimilated to constitute features of his own person, the individual is nevertheless not dependent for his final value and meaning on his people, but on God alone. 'The deepest and the most personal of what the human being is, he owes to God alone, and all that he owes to earthly communities, he owes because of God.'[42] 'There is in every human being a place which is free of earthly bonds, which

---

40 However, this does not mean, as it does in Aquinas, that the substance of the human being is formed in successive stages. Stein thinks the spiritual soul must exist from the earliest moment of the existence of the human being 'even if not yet expressing itself in actual, personally spiritual life'. Ibid., VII, IV.

41 Ibid., VIII, I, 3.

42 Ibid., VIII, III, 3.

does not come from other human beings and is not determined by other human beings.'[43] Just as a person can be called to put all his powers at the service of his people, he can also be called on his own. 'From the order of salvation it becomes clear that even a completely separate life, cut off from the world, can be fruitful for humanity.'[44]

Chapter IX: 'Transition from the Philosophical to the Theological View of Human Beings', examines the ways in which philosophical anthropology must be completed by theological anthropology. Because anthropology relies on ethics to furnish it with criteria for judging the relative importance of humanity, people and individuals, and furthermore because such criteria are explained and justified in theology in a manner more easily accessible than in philosophy, educational anthropology remains dependent on theological anthropology. Only the latter will render anthropology so complete that it gives sufficient reasons for the education (*Aufbau*) of the human person because only it accounts for and justifies its infinite value in relation to the Absolute.

***

We have seen that *The Structure of the Human Person* marks a high point from which Stein's entire work can be surveyed. It develops an educational theory at the confluence of phenomenology and metaphysics, underlining at the same time the inter-subjective constitution of the human person and her dependence on God alone for her final destination. The work also provides a privileged outlook on and contemporary criticism of the Nazi German ideology of the 'people'. And finally, the work insists that anthropology is the key to education while at the same time proposing just such an anthropology for discussion. This anthropology, however, cannot be completed without truths revealed about the human person, truths affirming and making intelligible what can be understood only confusedly by natural reason. By knowing the structure of the human person in its essential openness to a theological completion, we know, as much as natural

43   Ibid.
44   Ibid.

reason allows us to, what the person can do and be supposed to do. The role of the educator is to empower the human being to take charge of his or her own education and build up the human person in him- or herself and, because it cannot be done except in reciprocity, in his or her others. Education is thus, according to Stein, everyone's task, just as, and because, becoming a human person also is.

CHAPTER 8

Woman

Being a woman as well as being a man presents individuals with a task they share with only half of humanity. Because it is a task that probably essentially involves a relationship with those whose task it precisely is not, and also, accidentally so to speak, can free up incomparable creativity to the point of bringing children into the world, it is accompanied by joys and sorrows the depths of which stir every human heart and often break them. Whether the imbalance in existing reflections on gender, allowing for a disproportionate amount of reflection on woman compared to reflections on what it is to be a man in itself bears a message about reality or indeed is a misrepresentation of it, is a moot question. It remains that Stein's reflections on woman in fact also contain a philosophy of (male) man, although both remain somewhat embryonic, and also sometimes marked by not being worked out in the same philosophical depth as the rest of her philosophical anthropology.[1]

To discuss Stein's philosophy of woman, I wish in the following to describe its place within the context of the whole of Stein's philosophy (1). This will lead us to discuss the place of gender within the human person as Stein presents it in her early and later philosophical anthropology (2) and also the typical differences of the sexes as portrayed by Stein (3). Finally we

---

[1] Woman does not accurately reflect the texts assembled in the critical edition in Frau, which forms the basis for the present study. This work, however, must be read in the context not only of the contemporary lectures on education reprinted in Bildung but also in the context of the later concluding lectures from her time at the Marianum: Aufbau and Mensch. Unfortunately these important works are not yet translated into English. Marian Maskulak is preparing a translation for CWES of Aufbau.

shall be in a position to ask some questions concerning Stein's understanding of gender in its theological dimensions (4).

The place of the philosophy of woman within the whole of Stein's philosophy

Stein wrote about woman because she was asked to, not so much because she had an urge to do so. She did so at a time when she was working towards re-establishing a career in philosophy after having left it aside to teach German and Latin in the gymnasium for girls run by the Dominican nuns in Speyer. Requests for talks kept coming, and Stein kept answering these requests: in doing so she reached a very large public by means of a popular style of thought otherwise uncharacteristic of her. She never wrote a book on the topic, nor did gender figure prominently in her more substantial lectures on philosophical anthropology published as *The Structure of the Human Person* or indeed in its sequence *What is the human being?* Stein's 'philosophy of woman' is thus a prominent topic in her circumstantial writings – but it is not in any way her most substantial contribution to philosophy.

Her career as a lecturer on the issue took off in particular after she had given her 'The Ethos of Women's Professions' in Salzburg on 1 September 1930, at a meeting of the Association of Catholic Academics, the first of the annual 'Salzburgerwochen' (an institution still in existence). For this occasion she had first been offered to address the more fundamental topic of 'the Ethos of Christian Professions' something she said she accepted because 'that topic particularly attracted' her.[2] 'But then the people in Salzburg decided it was essential to address the women's theme separately, so I consented to change': Dietrich von Hildebrandt took over the other

2   Letter to Adelgundis Jägerschmidt, presumably July 1930, letter 57 in *Self Portrait in Letters*, CWES 5, ESGA II, letter 98, Juli/August 1930.

topic, and this process had given her food for thought.[3] She ended her talk in Salzburg in the following manner:

> I would like to raise a question that comes to mind again and again: the convention program clearly designates the various kinds of professions (the doctor, the priest, etc.). What need was there for a special category of women's professions? Besides, why are there such frequent discussions on women's professions but hardly any on men's professions? Is not man like woman aware of the coexistence and potential conflict between individual tendencies and masculine tendencies? Is it not also true of man that his nature is or should be a co-determining factor for the selection and formation of his vocation? Furthermore, do we not also here find the opposition between fallen and redeemed nature? I believe it would be very beneficial if at some time these questions would be considered seriously and thoroughly. For a wholesome collaboration of the sexes in professional life will be possible only if both achieve a calm and objective awareness of their nature and draw practical conclusions from it.[4]

The circumstantial nature of Stein's work on woman (ESGA 13 contains 10 more or less substantial articles on the topic, most of them solicited as a result of this first one) makes us look towards the motivation that existed among the public for asking her to deal with this particular topic. A brief glance at the times in which these lectures were solicited reveals that two weeks after her second lecture on the 'woman-question', on September 14 1930, 18.3 per cent of the votes were secured by the Nazi party during an election for the German Reichstag (which meant they got 107 deputies). The Nazi understanding that women had to play a role primarily in the home and as child bearers, which, to judge from this election result, had a significant amount of subscribers, together with the depression of 1929 issuing in massive unemployment figures, conspired to create an atmosphere where the question of women's professions, after the great victories of the women's movement in the first and second decade of the twentieth century, again became a real question. It was in fact this question that Stein was asked to address by her public, and she therefore rightly understood her

---

3   Ibid.
4   Woman, p. 57, translation adapted. Frau, p. 29.

lectures about woman as addressing a political question, 'eine brennende Gegenwartsfrage'.[5]

It was for Stein not only the reductionist Nazi subordination of women to the service of men in the private sphere, but also the competing 'Bolchevist' ideal of empty equality of all human beings reduced to their force of labour that needed correction. What was needed in order to counteract both and respond to the quest they grew from was the education of the whole, real human person, so that all, men and women alike, could reach their full human potential. To Stein the question of the education and professions of women highlighted the much more important question of the reality of the human being: the human being could not be a mere result of social factors shaping it arbitrarily for purposes that had nothing to do with its own being: conceiving it as such would create the highly unstable possibility of totalitarian exploitation, as indeed it in fact did. Gender, because it forms part of the concrete reality of the human being, thus provided an opportunity to argue that this reality would have to be taken into consideration and find an expression through the education and work offered for the development of the human being by society.

To Stein this reality meant first and foremost that women should be allowed to be educated *by* women (most education of girls in Germany was at the time in the hands of male teachers), so that women's potential *as* women could be reached, given the teachers' function as role model and their personal experience of living the life of a woman. That such education of the whole person (inclusive of gender and not despite it) was the best defence against both ideologies rests on the fact that each of these ideologies in their own way denied the particular being and value of the human being as such and of women in particular, instead understanding the being and value of human beings to rely on race, power, society or the force of labour. Education of the whole human being meant an affirmation of the dignity, person, humanity, gender and individuality of every human individual, i.e. also of women; and a challenge to the body, soul and personality of the individual. Since Stein in several cases was asked to

5   Frau, p. 1.

address the woman question in particular, a question she saw as reflecting this deeper political and moral problem, she addressed that question specifically, but always in a manner that pointed to the larger one of the education of the human person for its own good, the good of society, and for an eternal destiny.

Stein remained throughout her life interested in the human person, its relationship to its fellows, to communities, to the state and to religion. The philosophical anthropology developed in her early explicitly phenomenological period (*On the Problem of Empathy, Philosophy of Psychology and the Humanities, An Investigation Concerning the State* and *Introduction to Philosophy*) gave her a foundation for the lectures on woman. The popular nature of these latter however, means that they contain less sustained philosophical analysis and as a consequence make concessions to general opinion, which for the sake of brevity and political efficacy no doubt were necessary and indicated. For these reasons, perhaps, these lectures also made her famous, they were hotly debated and contested and are still widely read, probably because they are easy to read, much easier than Steins more substantial contributions to philosophy. They also give a rounded insight into a topic that is both highly personal and very context dependent. When Stein again obtained a foothold in academic work, she abandoned the topic, and in its place trod the systematic development of a Christian education theory based on a philosophical anthropology informed by her Catholic faith, a topic much closer to the centre of her natural interests.

Should we understand the lectures on woman as being opportunistic, therefore? That is probably stretching the argument too far: Stein ceased the opportunities handed to her with the intent of engaging fulltime in academic work again, she brought her political perspicacity to bear on the question which she addressed in a highly reflective manner still accessible to the non-philosopher, but her characteristic wisdom and profundity also gleams through the style of thought and reveals an earnest courage to put herself on the line in the concrete situation that was the overheated social climate of Germany in the thirties.

The place of gender within the human person

Let us thus, before we look closer at her understanding of female and male identity in these lectures, move to address the question of the role of gender within her philosophical anthropology, which forms the philosophical context of her well-known public appearances.

From her early works to the later twin-works *The Structure of the Human Person* and *What is the Human Being?* Stein's development as a philosopher is that of a phenomenologist who under the influence of Heidegger and Aquinas turns her attention increasingly towards being. Since she accorded eidetics an important place in her phenomenology the transition is one from formal ontology to material ontology – here concerning the human being. The continuity between her early work on the constitution of the human being in *On the Problem of Empathy* and her later philosophical anthropology is such that one can talk of the same ideas thought through in two complementary and convertible modes. The first mode unfolds amidst a conscious assessment of the complex web of social construction,[6] the second mode is supported by the teachings of the Catholic Church (understood by Stein to occupy a privileged place in the web of social construction because of its relation to Christ). The place of gender in the early and in the later anthropology reflects this convertibility.

In *On the Problem of Empathy* Stein uses the word 'type' to designate that *as which* the 'I' sees itself, in so far as it sees itself as of the same kind as the 'you'.[7] This type is not fixed, but can be varied, even at will, in the same way as eidetic variation involves wilfully re-imagining the entity under investigation in order to assess its limits. I am thus able to conceive myself as fulfilling various types; 'person', 'human individual', 'woman', 'lecturer', 'member of the Irish Philosophical Society', each of which captures me under a certain aspect. I can indeed also see myself as 'animal' or 'thing', which captures still more basic aspects of me. In Stein's early work the

6   See Part I.
7   PE, III, 5, in particular (b).

'type' is that according to which I interpret the experience of 'you' and 'I' as analogous, and hence the means by which my world as socially constructed is constituted as objective. The type or types I take to be mine define who co-constitutes my world. Woman and man are thus types according to which I constitute myself in the world and according to which I compile and compare my experience from and with others of the same type. It is normal and rational to think that the types of 'woman' and 'man' fit into the more general type of the human being or person (since the species of human beings comprise two sexes), but normality or rationality are both normative for constitution, and nothing can force constitution if it isn't occurring or thought to ought to occur. This means that although constitution inclusive of the two genders is normal and seen as such it may not occur. What may occur instead could rely on one type rather than another, so that the human implicitly is reduced to one of the genders.[8]

What the content of the types of man and woman are, however, apart from them being possible forms according to which the I can identify itself, is not made clear in Stein's early work. A means of distinguishing them from 'social types' (which she later will explore) seems absent: 'age, sex, occupation, station, nationality, generation' are all considered 'general experiential structures to which the individual is subordinate', and in fact distinguished by their pertaining to the spiritual realm as distinct from the natural realm.[9] Such experiential structures may erect boundaries: 'I cannot fulfil what conflicts with my own experiential structure. But I can still have it given in the manner of empty representation'.[10] This means that if I identify with a type that excludes another (as 'man' and 'woman' might) I will have to put imagination to work to emptily represent that which 'my' type excludes, and it will not be something 'I am', as it is with my own type. As experiential structure is also the presupposition for the

---

8   For further reflection on Stein's understanding of 'type' see my *On the Problem of Human Dignity*, pp. 252–6.

9   PE, IV, 7 (b). That means they are spiritual realities, not natural ones as indeed all ideas and concepts are: the latter being products of a spiritual process, meant to understand natural reality.

10   Ibid.

formation of communities, my 'type' also determines the types of communities to which I can belong.[11]

Sixteen years later, in *The Structure of the Human Person* (1932) Stein does distinguish between social types and the inborn predispositions which are ultimately shape the person from within his or her self-constitution. She sees the inborn types as being those of the human, the gender, the specific and the individual, so that these types discovered in each individual are fundamental to the social types, which in turn reform what is already formed.[12] Education, in other words, does not invent the human being: it forms it in accordance with a pre-established individual programme, visible and intuitable in the individual human being whose humanity, gender, specificity and individuality gives him or her concrete dimensions. She tentatively calls gender a part-species (*Teilspecies*), in which individuals find themselves from birth. But then she says the following:

> The male and the female specificity (männliche und weibliche Eigenart) is something that must first unfold to actuality in the course of a life; that happens again under the influence of the environment, and so is, in all later stages of development, that which meets us and which could be designated as the 'manly' or the 'womanly', probably a social type, in which what is determined by 'the environment' and the 'specificity' fundamental to the social formation are very difficult to distinguish. (Thus is explained the quarrel over whether male and female gender are specific differences, i.e. fundamental to social formation, or whether they are only typical, i.e. results of social formation.)[13]

'Man' and 'woman' are in other words types, the natural foundation of which is lost in constitution, as this happens against the background of the spiritual achievements we call culture. We thus only know what it is now, and how it matters now, and that only provisionally, and in so far as it really matters to us.

---

11   PPH. II, 4 (a). Hence the importance of the identifying with the type of the human being, as discussed in Chapter 6.

12   Aufbau, VIII, II, 4.

13   Ibid., own translation.

The typical differences as perceived by Stein

This point must be kept in mind when we read the slightly earlier popular lectures on woman. It justifies the view that these lectures must be seen as a political intervention, indeed as Stein's most consciously political intervention, her strategic attempt to counteract the influence of Nazism on what she regarded the most holy of tasks: education. That gender is both presupposed for its social interpretation and a result of it means that any theorising about it is observation as much as it is proposal. From this stems the difficulty of talking about the subject.

The double basic difference between the sexes that Stein most often returns to, and thus both observes and proposes to observe, is that of men being primarily focussed on the factual (*Sachliches*) in a life that develops specific talents (or one specific talent) to the point of excellence at the expense of other talents and a sense of the wholeness of the person, while women focus primarily on the personal and have an urge towards developing the entire person (in themselves and in others) in a harmonious manner, sometimes at the expense of maximum development of specific talents. Thus she will for example say the following in her 'Woman's Value in National Life' (14 April 1928, given to *the association of women teachers in Bayern*):

> Man appears more *objective*: it is natural for him to dedicate his faculties to a discipline (be it mathematics or technology, a trade or business management) and thereby to subject himself to the precepts of this discipline. *Woman's attitude is personal*; and this has several meanings: in one instance she is happily involved with her total being in what she does; then she has particular interest for the living, concrete person, and indeed, as much for her own personal life and personal affairs as for those of other persons.
>
> Through submission to a discipline, man easily experiences a *one-sided development*. In woman, there lives a natural drive towards totality and self-containment. And, again, this drive has a twofold direction: she herself would like to become a *complete human being*, one who is fully developed in every way; and she would like to help others to become so, and by all means, she would like to do justice to the complete human being wherever she has to deal with persons.[14]

14   Woman, p. 255.

The flipside to these positive characteristics of both sexes, are certain exaggerations, which Stein attributes to the Fall. For the man this flipside is an exaggeration of the objective attitude: a tendency to dominate and bring not only his own forces but also those of his surroundings, and in particular those of his wife, to serve his particular purpose (the purpose which he himself also serves), which often is too small or too particular for the human beings involved to flourish. This purpose, indeed, does not make any sense, if it were not because it was dictated by the further purpose of the flourishing of the human person. The result of his drive towards objectivity, efficiency and domination is thus often instrumentalisation.

For the woman the flipside is an overemphasis of the personal. This can take the form of an exaggerated interest in the self, its moods, desires and tastes; it can also take the form of curiosity, the exaggerated (but superficial) interest in everything personal pertaining to the other (gossip); and it can finally take the form of domination, in which case it mostly happens by means of manipulation: emotional or motivational.

> Excess of interest in both her own and in the other's personality merge in feminine surrender, the urge to lose herself completely in a human being; but in so doing, she does justice neither to self nor to the humanity of the other, and at the same time, becomes unfit for exercising other duties.[15]

The final, and most lethal (to herself) flipside of woman's specificity is thus her tendency to surrender herself completely to another human being. If this other human being is a man who displays the flipside of the male, he will encourage the surrender in order to dominate, and the characteristic disaster of many human relationships thus spins out of control.

Although Stein does not propose a 'cure' for the masculine overemphasis on the objective, except the reflection on its value, we might feel free to think it would involve the conscious exercise of empathy and involvement in all areas where a personal attitude is particularly called for: childrearing, understanding of personal relationships, seeing things from other people's perspectives, and thus gaining an understanding of the particular

---

15   Woman, p. 257, translation adapted. Frau, p. 5.

role (and indeed of the particularity of the pursuit) that one's own task has in a greater whole.

Stein does, however, propose a cure for the feminine overemphasis on the personal (and given the political scope of the lectures, we cannot be too surprised):

> A good natural method for this [overemphasis] is thoroughly objective work. Every work, no matter of what kind, whether housework, a trade, science or anything else, necessitates submitting to the laws of the matter concerned; the whole person, thoughts, just as all moods and dispositions, must be made subordinate to the work. And whoever has learned this, has become objective, has lost something of the hyper-individuality and has attained a definite freedom of self; at the same time she has attained an inner depth – she has attained a basis of self-control.[16]

Questions concerning Stein's understanding of gender in its theological dimensions

Stein admits of a 'certain precedence' of man over woman, which she bases on her understanding of Catholic doctrine.[17] She claims this precedence stems from two facts: that man was created before woman and that Christ became a man, born of a woman. But both of these arguments can be turned on their head, as the fact that the animals were created before man does not make them superior, and as God might have chosen the least favoured to shame the stronger. The arguments, however, must have had a symbolic value in Stein's surroundings so that the signal she sends by using them slots into a contemporary discourse and set of expectations. Dominant Theologians, Christians, Nazis and Conservatives alike might have seen this 'certain precedence' as the backbone of the known world order, and

16 Ibid.
17 'Beruf des Mannes und der Frau nach Natur- und Gnadenordnung' in Frau p. 59, 62; Woman p. 61, 65. See also 'Probleme der neueren Mädchenbildung', Frau p. 175.

would have challenged Stein had they not heard them there. Stein was not a revolutionary – she was much too cautious about sudden social changes for that (women had only obtained the vote in 1919, three years after she defended her doctoral dissertation, and she was now observing how many women contributed towards bringing the Nazis to power). Moreover, Stein had a message – that of the importance of education, education of the whole person, man and woman as concrete individuals and gendered human beings exposed to each other and to each other's opinions about each other – which mattered more to her. By it she attempted to preserve the possibility of adequate education in the future, even by the means of providing arguments relying for their validity on popular acclaim.

Stein balanced this stated precedence against a certain superiority of women over men as regards the ability to be united with God: she claimed women's capacity for surrender prepared them particularly well for this union.[18] Here again, we may question whether a soldier's very male surrender to the fight under orders does not exemplify surrender just as much as the woman's does. It is of no less consequence for the one involved – in both cases individual life is lost to a foreign will whose superiority is embraced. Also, the Christian heritage presents us with the example of the surrender of Christ, the man, to the Father's will, a surrender which surely is no less valid than that of Mary's, although it may engage our sexual imagination less well.

It remains a fact, perhaps, that Stein attempted, in these her most political interventions, to catch the prevalent (sexual) imagination and make it work toward a goal that in the circumstances may well have been regarded by Stein as justifying the means: the goal of education, the education of both sexes by both sexes, as human persons and human beings, the eternal destiny of which far outweigh their importance as gendered beings. This

---

18   E.g. Frau p. 77; FEB p. 514/ EES, p. 430. She also, and perhaps more importantly, regarded the relation between mother and child as the purest of human relationships, their archetype. The mother is superior, of course, only in the sense that she is not superior, and her relation with her children relies precisely on this enabling putting herself at their disposal. That there can be precedence in putting oneself last also is the message of the Gospel.

goal includes for Stein the relativisation of sexual imagination for the sake of the constitution of the human being on the type of the human person. But to reach it takes time and patience. And it is this latter fact that may explain her use of these arguments.

It is interesting to note that in Stein's theological anthropology, which assembles all the dogmatic declarations that can elucidate the question of the book's title: *What is the Human Being?*, gender plays no role at all: Stein seems to have been unable (or unwilling?) to find any dogmatic declarations about the issues.[19]

***

What we can learn from Stein's philosophy of woman (and man) is first and foremost that gender remains a feature of the concrete real human person, but that this person's importance far outweighs the importance of gender. Gender is in some sense a transitory focus, a changing type that allows for the building of individuality and occupies a definite place in the structure of the individual human person. Its significance, however, must remain subordinate to that of the human being and that of the person, which alone constitute types that allow for the formation of the whole human being. This again may mean that we in fact cannot know exactly what it is to be a man, or to be a woman: both express a relational dimension of the human being, its standing in relation to something other than itself, which may not ultimately be intelligible in its specificity if it has no fixed content independent of cultural construction. If masculinity and femininity have content along the lines given by Stein (the high versus the whole development, the objective versus the personal attitude), these seem to serve the purpose of enabling correction rather than justifying concrete development. The polarities seem proposed for our consideration to halt the development of attitudes that ultimately are detrimental to the human person as such, whether as such or as living in community with others.

---

19 Mensch is a string of quotations from Denzinger, i.e. dogmatic declarations from close to 2000 years of Church history, all relating to who the human being is.

In so far as gender in fact is an intermediate type that may take the place of the identification of the whole human being, it is no coincidence that Stein does not engage the issue of sexual difference in her substantial philosophical works. That gender is a subordinate issue, however, does not mean that it is without importance to address it, and that this is required whenever the opposition between the sexes is so disturbed as to inflame the imagination of whole peoples and stir them into stereotypical action, in a manner that inevitably is destructive since it falls short of enabling the education and development of the whole of the human person.

CHAPTER 9

Phenomenology and Thomism

It is generally known that Stein was a non-believing Jew before her conversion to Catholicism. She encountered Aquinas as a way into the Catholic tradition. Her translation-commentary on *De veritate*, which came out after many years of work in 1931 and 1932, afforded her the time to habituate herself to his thought world – and with it to the Catholic worldview. She 'became so absorbed by his thought that an inner clash between it and the phenomenological way of philosophising was inevitable.'[1] Her own first formation was as a phenomenologist, first studying with and later being the assistant of Husserl in Göttingen and Freiburg. During this time both Adolph Reinach and Max Scheler had a profound influence on her, and each in their own way prepared her for the encounter with the thoughts of Thomas Aquinas.

Scheler and Reinach's version of phenomenology was, like that of Husserl's *Ideas*, marked by the exploration of the intuition of essences. They shared the understanding that an important task for the discipline of phenomenology is to enable such intuition,[2] which is not exhausted in the achievement of definitions, but rather commands a sustained effort at describing, discerning and clarifying, in order to look afresh and let the phenomena *show themselves forth* in their purity. The purpose is insight – *Wesenschau*. When Husserl's transcendental turn led him to practically

---

1   A fragmentary foreword to *Potency and Act* is found in 'German Editor's Introduction' in *Potency and Act*, trans. W. Redmond, CWES vol. XI, p. xxvi.

2   See for example Adolph Reinach, 'Concerning Phenomenology', trans. Dallas Willard, *The Personalist* 50 (1969), pp. 194–221, reprinted in *The Phenomenology Reader*, eds D. Moran and T. Mooney (London and New York: Routledge, 2002) pp. 180–96.

support Heidegger as his successor, Reinach came, for the Bergzabern phenomenologisits, to 'stand for' – posthumously – the analysis of essences.[3]

Stein, like Husserl, understood ultimate intuitability to be 'transcendental', and did not see that as conflicting with Reinach's designation of the realm as 'a priori', a term she also sometimes used herself.[4] Her understanding of the transcendental I as a pole of experience is one she shared with all the phenomenologists. In so far as she analysed experience from this point of view she must be called a transcendental phenomenologist. We could, however, just as easily call her a realist phenomenologist, if we mean by that that she, like other early phenomenologists, insists on the importance of eidetic analysis for completing the phenomenological project, and understand the world to be given as real in contrast with essences and essentialities, the being of which is essential (*Wesenhaftes*).

A guiding question in Stein's approach to Thomas was in fact that of the transcendental dimension of knowledge (*Erkenntnis*). She had become habituated to the Cartesian starting point and was very familiar with the Kantian intuition of the synthetic *a priori* as structuring for knowledge. She had found in Husserl a methodical approach to take account of these modern insights, anchoring them in transcendental experience. She found it difficult to renounce an eidetic analysis of knowledge.[5] Her reading of Aquinas was to find another way of approaching the transcendental dimension of knowledge, rooted in the necessity of affirming being as an intrinsic

---

3   The excellent work of Jean Hering, 'Bemerkungen über das Wesen, die Wesenheit und die Idee', *Jahrbuch für Philosophie und phänomenologische Forschung* 1921, pp. 495–543 clarifies how the terms were used among the (early) phenomenologists, and does so by application of the method of eidetic analysis itself. For a superb introduction to the Bergzabern Phenomenologists and their understanding of Heidegger's influence, see Joachim Feldes: 'A yet hidden story: Edith Stein and the Bergzabern Circle' in the proceedings of the first IASPES conference, ed. Haydn Gurmin and Mette Lebech (Nordhausen: Traugott Bautz, forthcoming).

4   Beiträge, p. 9, for her (very infrequent) use of the word 'transzendental', Einfühlung, p. 114 and Beiträge, p. 200, for her use of 'a priori'.

5   ESGA 23, p. 3 ('Vorbemerkung').

part of the scientific endeavour inherited from Aristotle and issuing in a full sketch of the dimensions of a *Seinslehre*.[6]

We shall follow this question of the transcendental dimension of knowledge from its first formulation in the dialogue Stein wrote for the *Festschrift* marking Husserl's seventieth birthday (1), through her treatment of the First Question of *De veritate* (2) and her investigation of *Potency and Act* (3) to *Finite and Eternal Being*'s admittance of truth as the transcendental quality of being which reveals the Trinitarian analogy of being, articulated in natural being, finite spirit and infinite spirit (4).

As Stein progressed from phenomenology through ontology to metaphysics she had a very important fellow traveller, who became her Godmother when she was baptised in 1922: Hedwig Conrad-Martius. Conrad-Martius was not, however, a Catholic, but a protestant Christian, nor was she particularly interested in Thomas Aquinas, but she was, from the beginning of her career as President of the Göttingen Philosophy Society, profoundly interested in ontology, and in particular in the ontology of the real (as distinct from the ideal), and that from a phenomenological perspective. Conrad-Martius insured that the question of a phenomenology of reality was always present to the minds of the early phenomenologists.[7] Stein's dialogue with Conrad-Martius was frank, serious and challenging. Their friendship accompanied Stein to maturity in a direction growing from the same root as herself: phenomenology.

Conrad-Martius survived the war, and published in 1957 an outstanding work called *Das Sein*[8] (*Being*), in which she presented the fruits of her

---

6   FEB, Foreword.

7   *Zur Ontologie und Erscheinungslehre der realen Aussenwelt*, in *Jahrbuch für Philosophie und Phaenomenologische Forschung*, 1916, pp. 345–542 and *Realontologie* equally in the *Jahrbuch*, but 1923, pp. 139–333. When one is crediting Heidegger with turning phenomenology towards ontology, one should not overlook that the immediate context into which he writes already dealt extensively with ontology. For a discussion of Conrad-Martius' Heidegger-critique see Alexandra Pfeiffer, *Hedwig Conrad-Martius. Eine Phänomenologische Sicht auf Natur und Welt* (Würzburg: Königshausen und Neumann, 2005) pp. 43–8.

8   (München: Kösel Verlag, 1957).

mature reflections.[9] The first part of *Das Sein* concerns categorical being, the being of states of affairs, something which had already interested Reinach in his theory of Negative Judgement. The insight common to both Conrad-Martius and Reinach is that the affirmation of being forms an integral part of the essence of judgement, such that no phenomenological analysis of the act of judging is possible without an inclusion of its correlate: being. Thus a phenomenological analysis of being should paradoxically be possible, and indeed necessary to complete the phenomenological project of founding the sciences.

Heidegger's way from phenomenology to fundamental ontology followed along a similar path. Conrad-Martius, however, was very critical of Heidegger's approach, which she, like Stein, understood to illegitimately reduce being to the human being (Stein thought it reduced it to the being of the unredeemed human being).[10] To Conrad-Martius being could not be thus arbitrarily limited to the human being because judgement concerns cosmic (natural) being and also infinite or eternal being besides that of the human being. Stein's criticism of Heidegger can be found in an appendix to *Finite and Eternal Being*, and her engagement with Conrad-Martius' thought pervades both *Potency and Act* and *Finite and Eternal Being*. Both are facts that prove that this impetus towards ontology stemming from within the phenomenological tradition already blew like a strong wind in the sails of Stein as she engaged with Thomas Aquinas' thought. She was convinced that the subjects with which Aquinas was dealing ultimately had to be the same as those of her times, and thus she read him not as a historian of philosophy would, but as a philosopher does: for the arguments he presents and in order to encounter a perspective to challenge her own.

Erich Przywara SJ, who in the years after her baptism had a mentoring function for Stein, was indeed, in contrast with Conrad-Martius, a Catholic. Stein takes pains in the foreword to *Finite and Eternal Being* to carefully

9   Stein responded to both *Metaphysische Gespräche* (1921) and *Realontologie* (1923) in
      PA and FEB.
10   ESGA 11–12, Anhang I: Martin Heideggers Existentialphilosophie, p. 480, HA
      p. 81. See also Chapter 11.

explain the relationship between his *Analogia entis* (1932) and her own work, implying she has read it in great detail. The most important difference seems to be in their understanding of the role of theology for metaphysics, a topic discussed at length in the *Introduction* to *Finite and Eternal Being*, part 4, entitled 'The meaning and possibility of a Christian Philosophy'.

The most fundamental problem Stein would retain with Aquinas' thought through to *Finite and Eternal Being* was that matter should be the principle of individuation.[11] This problem is linked to our general problem of the transcendental structure of knowledge in that the Aristotelian view reserves a transcendental place for the non-intelligible (matter), something Stein would explain to be unnecessary for the redeemed worldview, in which everything is potentially intelligible in the Word.[12] Apart from such a structural commitment to an idea of pure matter as being in principle non-intelligible[13] there seems to be no teaching of Thomas she did not assimilate, but it must be stressed that that is exactly what she did: *assimilate* Aquinas' thought. Her worldview was very much her own, and still very much that of a phenomenologist in her mature years. One would not be able to say that she is *not* (also) a Thomist – but whether one would

---

11   Borden Sharkey, *Thine Own Self* also affirms this, but argues that what Stein puts in its stead, 'individual forms', has no advantages compared to Aquinas' solution, maybe even disadvantages. Stein does think that the individual has an essence, and that essences have essential being, but form and essence are not synonyms for Stein (nor are they indeed for Aristotle). Some of Borden Sharkey's argument relies on an Aristotelian/Thomistic reading of Stein's concept of essence to which the *a priori* (transcendental) nature of essential being remains incomprehensible. This is because the understanding of the transcendental realm of essences can only be accessed from within phenomenologically purified experience as that which informs and structures it. Stein's focus is on the one hand on the individual, in the same way as Aristotle's focus was on *ousia* because it is that without which the world remains unintelligible. On the other hand it is on essences of greater or lesser generality. This is another way of expressing what Borden Sharkey rightly affirms that Stein's concern is not with *individuation*, but with *individuality* (p. 18).

12   FEB, IV, §4, 5.

13   One could say she reserves a place for understanding matter as unintelligible, namely as characteristic of the unredeemed worldview.

actually want to call her one, would depend on what one understands by Thomism.[14] One might understand Thomism as a doctrine in which Act and Potency, Form and Matter present definitive formative and fundamental concepts, the meaning and function of which is beyond question. Or one could understand Thomism to be a doctrine, which relies on the best available philosophy for interpreting the world with the help of Revelation to form a view of the whole that allows for science to be possible. According to the first view, as we shall see, Stein is not a Thomist. According to the second she is.[15]

The *Festschrift* article

On the occasion of Husserl's seventieth birthday, a *Festschrift* was prepared for him by his students and associates. The first version of the article Stein contributed presents Aquinas in a dialogue with Husserl on the eve of the latter's birthday.[16] It was later rewritten at the instigation of the editor of

14   See Borden Sharkey, *Thine Own Self*, pp. xvii–xx: 'Edith Stein and Thomism' for the various points of view that have been expressed on the matter.

15   It would be awkward to call Stein's philosophy 'scholastic', except if what one means by that is simply 'academic', i.e. conducted in the 'Schools', i.e. in or around the institutional setting of the University. But this would include most contemporary philosophy, which would jar with the implicit understanding that 'scholastic' refers to a type of philosophy conducted within a specific time period past (however one defines this period), which, as it happens, accepted faith as a source of knowledge. Stein does accept faith as a source of knowledge, but that seems nevertheless insufficient to characterise the thought as 'scholastic', except if one believes that the tradition of scholastic philosophy is not restricted to the past. See Borden Sharkey, *Thine own Self*, pp. 56–72: 'The Scholastic and Phenomenological Traditions'.

16   The title of the published article was 'Husserl and Aquinas, a Comparison', 1929. The first version of the article, 'Was ist Philosophie? Ein Gespräch zwischen Edmund Husserl und Thomas von Aquino', was published first in Edith Stein, *Erkenntnis und Glaube*, Edith Steins Werke = ESW (the first Herder edition of Stein's works),

the *Festschrift*, Martin Heidegger, to omit the dialogue form, but retain all the points. As Stein in the first version portrays the characters of her interlocutors as well as their philosophical divergences, this version is enriched by the wealth of information one gathers from an attitude displayed by a character.[17] Stein's familiarity with her characters is obtained from her engagement with the work of both authors, and in the case of Husserl, also through personal acquaintance. The characters present her understanding of their ideal selves engaging in a dialogue the basis of which lies outside time. Stein's Aquinas (SAquinas) has a clear grasp of what distinguishes his position from Husserl's, and moreover has the benefit of hindsight of more than 700 years. This allows him to explain his position to Husserl, and also at times to explain Husserl's position to Husserl. Since the article is addressed to Husserl as a gift, it is mostly Aquinas that Stein lets speak, possibly to avoid phrases Husserl would find alienating. The interpretation of his thought by his student Stein is thus voiced by SAquinas, but whether a Thomist would find this Aquinas an accurate intellectual portrayal is a moot question. Stein's Husserl (SHusserl), in contrast, sometimes will not discuss a point or loses himself in thought to the point where an answer is not forthcoming. Such foibles must have been clear enough to all and also to Husserl, for him not to be offended by their humoristic portrayal. Alternatively, Stein is making a point (which Heidegger as an editor might have wanted to mitigate). The impression is of two characters genuinely attempting to understand each other's viewpoints in a highly complex but serene debate.

The dialogue starts out with Aquinas affirming his accord with Husserl in philosophy having to be done 'as a rigorous science', as a 'serious, sober

---

Bd. XV (Freiburg – Basel – Vienna: Herder, 1993). It has appeared recently in ESGA 9 as the last of the ESGA volumes. The two versions were translated into English and helpfully presented alongside each other for comparison by the translator and editor Walther Redmond, in Edith Stein: *Knowledge and Faith*, CWES 8, pp. 1–63.

17   Erich Przywara also appreciated the 'artistic value' of this piece. 'Edith Stein. Zu ihrem zehnten Todestag' in *In und Gegen* (Nuremberg: Glock und Lutz, 1955), quoted in Andreas Speer und Francesco Tommasi: 'Einleitung' in *Thomas von Aquin, Über die Wahrheit 1* (ESGA 23), p. XXI.

inquiry of reason.'[18] Then five important points of divergence are identified and the position of both thinkers on these points is discussed. The points are (1) the role of faith in philosophy, (2) the need for a starting point for philosophical inquiry, (3) the relationship between the I and the absolute I, (4) empirical and/or eidetic methods and (5) the nature of intuition.

(1) For SAquinas faith is necessary for the completion of the work of reason, so that philosophy as a rigorous science cannot be completed without it. SHusserl, in contrast, objects that a distinction between natural and supernatural reason would jar with the transcendentality of philosophy, where such distinctions have no place. SAquinas, however, finding ways to understand and take SHusserl's perspective, reproaches SHusserl for not seeing the (essential) limits of human reasoning, which condemns our philosophy to be fragmentary. SAquinas intimates that this fragmentation can be overcome only with the help of faith. SHusserl retorts he never intended to contest the right of faith within religion, but denies it can play any decisive role in philosophy. Thus the distinction between natural and supernatural reason is accepted by him, and SAquinas is able to follow up by introducing a corresponding distinction between natural and supernatural philosophy: metaphysics relying on both. On metaphysics relying on both, he comments in a parenthesis:

> (The loss of the appreciation for this fact accounts for the abstruse character of all modern philosophy and at the same time, quite consistently, for the mistrust of metaphysics felt by so many modern thinkers.)[19]

It remains that the certitude of faith is a question of faith, and thus that modern philosophy is justified in its mistrust if it does not want to rely on

---

18   Stein, *Knowledge and Faith*, p. 8.
19   This is SAquinas' explanatory comment. *Knowledge and Faith* op. cit. p. 19. He continues a bit later: 'I should add, by the way, that you will find scarcely anything of what I have just been saying about the relation of faith and reason in my writings. For me it was all a self-evident starting-point. I am speaking now from a later reflection on how I actually proceed, as it is needed today for a rapprochement with moderns' p. 20.

it. SAquinas clearly has an understanding of this, but he is equally insistent that metaphysics cannot achieve its goal without faith.

(2) Thus the question of whether there is a need for a starting-point in philosophy presents itself. To SAquinas it is clear that modern philosophers, who exclude faith and make do with natural knowledge, must first search for a starting-point for their inquiry. He presents Husserl's quest for a realm of genuine immanence within the transcendentally purified consciousness as prolonging this quest for a knowledge that is absolutely certain, absolutely one with its object. But he does not think this quest can succeed without faith in God, who *is* this knowledge identical with is object. The quest is not fruitless, however. It leads to a 'methodological purity, perhaps unknown before.'[20] As he contemplates it, SAquinas admits his dependence on the methods of his time and confesses his ultimate intentions of serving truth and peoples' peace of mind. His is a 'philosophy for life.'[21]

(3) It is thus on the issue of first truth, on the relation between the pure (or transcendental) I and the absolute I, that their philosophies must part ways. SAquinas explains how Husserl's transcendental phenomenology *is* general ontology, but 'with a radical shift of sign' and admits there is room in his own philosophy for accommodating constitutional analyses – i.e. analyses of how things are constituted for consciousness – but not as fundamental. SHusserl, however, does not wish to enter into a discussion of the difference between the ego and God, but is far from admitting defeat.[22]

(4) Instead he changes the topic and wishes to ask how SAquinas views the distinction between essence and fact, since it is fundamental to ontology as SHusserl understands it (material and regional ontologies investigating the essence of the various subjects of the sciences, under which the facts sort). SAquinas admits he 'did not distinguish [essence and fact] as a matter of methodological principle.'[23] What he was after was the broadest possible picture of *this* world and indeed of it as the basis for the

20   Ibid., p. 24.
21   Ibid., pp. 27–8.
22   Ibid., pp. 32–3.
23   Ibid., p. 34.

best action (a motive SAquinas also explicitly ascribes to SHusserl). But he did distinguish between essence and accident and considered that which applies to things according to their essence as the 'basic scaffolding of the world'.[24] Although the play of free possibilities was not his concern, eidetic analyses conducted through such variation were granted by SHusserl's students to scholastic enquiries according to SAquinas, and it allowed them to access the latter.

(5) And thus we come to the last discussion concerning intuition or essence-viewing (*Wesenschau*), which is the longest of them all. An immediate vision of essence seems to be available to Husserl as *a priori*. About it SAquinas states that *Wesenschau* 'may well have been the greatest stumbling block in your philosophy for Kantians and neo-scholastics' alike.'[25] Such immediacy as regards the knowledge of essences obtains only for the blessed in Heaven or indeed for God, according to SAquinas. On the other hand, it also obtains for our knowledge of principles.[26] SAquinas is not keen to admit such immediate (*a priori*) knowledge to essences in *statu via*, but admits they may be obtained through reasoning, such as for example eidetic variation. But the knowledge of them is mediate in another sense, it is mediated through *species*. 'Knowledge of the species themselves, on the other hand, is not knowledge through species. But it is still mediate in the first sense of being acquired actively.'[27] Thus SAquinas is open to the possibility of phenomenological essences being equivalent to the species through which we gain knowledge of things, and as knowledge of the species is reflexive, it is immediate in that it is not mediated through species. Only the blessed can intuit this fully, as they do so in the Word whom they see face to face (and see the world through). For us in *statu via*, the intuition of essence is never completely fulfilled, although it helps us clarify our understanding. It remains that for us the intuition of essence is immediate in two senses (only): it is *not* known through effects, and it

24   Ibid., p. 36.
25   Ibid., p. 39.
26   Ibid., p. 50.
27   Ibid., p. 56.

is *not* empty. This is very little in comparison to the intuition of essence being completely fulfilled.

It may well be that this last question concerning intuition is what allows for the most fruitful interaction between phenomenologists and Thomists. Possibly it is the fundamental one involving the rest, as it also touches on the relationship between the essences and the Ideas, and therefore also on the relationship between the human I and God.

The translation-commentary of *De veritate*

Stein had thus outlined the differences between the two standpoints she set out to bridge and integrate.[28] She continues this integration in a new key in her translation-commentary of *De veritate*, which also bears the title: 'Aquinas' teaching on Knowledge according to the *Quaestiones de veritate*'[29] – a systematic title truer to her intentions to penetrate to the meaning of what Aquinas says by means of her 'translation'. To this end Thomas' text is restructured, abbreviated and provided with succinct and insightful résumés and critical comments, attempting to penetrate – as always – into the matters under discussion (the things themselves) and not only into what Thomas says.

This way of proceeding – successful only because of its meticulous precision – highlights the epochal difference between the presuppositions of classical and modern philosophy.[30] The thoroughness lets Stein 'discover'

---

28 'Wenn es nur ein Kern von Wahrheit hier und dort ist, so muss es auch eine Brücke geben'. ESGA 23, p. 4. The 'Vorbemerkung' is found in Stein's *Handexemplar*, where she has inserted it in her own handwriting, and reconstructed carefully by the editors.

29 Ibid., p. 3.

30 A publication of the work as a translation has occurred (Wiesbaden: Marixverlag 2013 (Kindle)) with a foreword of Bruno Kern. He presents the work in the introduction ('Von der Vollkommenheit der Geschöpfe gering denken heißt die Vollkommenheit der göttlichen Macht herabmindern') in the following manner: 'Die Textabschnitte

things obvious to the careful and persistent reader, which easily evaporates when doctrinal consistency takes precedence. Aquinas, for instance, taught in fact that God and angels do have knowledge of the individual, something which reveals that he thought that individuation by matter (by the principle of non-intelligibility) did not matter to them.[31] Thus individuality as such cannot be unintelligible (and he could not reasonably have thought it was) since it is not unintelligible to superior intellects. Insofar as he thought that the true is what being is in relation to knowledge, and that being is the first object of the intellect (i.e. that which it primarily knows), no being can in fact be in principle unintelligible.[32] This transcendental insight about knowledge and about being remains the stepping stone for Stein from phenomenology to Thomist ontology since it constitutes the transcendental core of being, knowledge and truth.

Potency and Act

Because we know that *Finite and Eternal Being* resulted from Stein's rewriting of *Potency and Act* for publication, we are tempted to read the latter as an earlier version of the former. That is helpful in so far as the latter work is, according to the subtitle, 'studies toward a philosophy of being' and seeks, like *Finite and Eternal Being*, to ascend to the meaning of being. The two

---

der einzelnen Artikel sind so zusammengestellt, dass der Grundgedanke und die wesentlichen Argumentationsschritte leicht nachvollziebar werden und die Leser und Leserinnen sich nicht in einem Labyrinth unterschiedlicher Argumentationsketten verlieren. Mit guten Überleitungen fügen sich die Texte so aneinander, dass der Hauptgedanke klar hervortritt. Jede Questio wird mit einer äußerst erhellenden Zusammenfassung der wesentlichen Gedanken beschlossen.' This edition might well allow the work to be read in the manner in which it was intended, as an introduction to Aquinas' own thought.

31   DV, Q. VIII, a. 11. Aquinas: *De veritate* Q. VIII, a. 11.
32   DV, Q. 1 a. 1.

works are, however, profoundly different. The concepts of form and matter as structural features present in the first work have been superseded in the second and no longer serve to account for the difference between regional (material) and formal ontology. Since *Potency and Act* issues in the insight that being as such cannot be treated in a purely formal way by means of formal ontology alone, but in fact is simultaneously a matter of content, in need of treatment in material ontologies, this distinction is given up in the later work, which concentrates on the *meaning* of being.

Potency and Act is an attempt to clarify what potency and act mean, from within experience (i.e. phenomenologically), and in accordance with both Aquinas' and Husserl's use of the terms. Apart from understanding what those terms mean (i.e. conducting an eidetic analysis of them), Stein is exploring their role for Thomas's and Husserl's understanding of the whole, of all there is to know, of being. She says herself that her work issues from an attempt to understand the 'method' of Aquinas, to expose the *Organon* of his fundamental concepts, something she also struggled with in her early comparison/dialogue.[33] She finds it necessary to do so because Thomas does not explore his own method, and because she, as a philosopher, must find out whether the reliance on these terms is justified or not. Her own method is thus an 'objective' (*sachliche*) analysis of Aquinas' fundamental concepts, i.e. an investigation of the realities expressed in the concepts, a penetration into their meaning, into 'the things themselves' in order to assess the validity of the concepts.[34] As potency and act divide and concern being in its entirety, penetration towards their meaning is likewise a way of approaching the whole of being, as indeed Aquinas did with the help of this distinction, following a well-established tradition.

In the work we see being occurring under three forms – the internal world, the external world and the beyond of the world. This corresponds to the spirit in persons and ideas, nature in material things, and the absolute as that towards which both of these point for the explanation of their existence. Both of the latter announce themselves in the first in virtue of

---

33   PA, p. 1.
34   PA, pp. 9–11.

their transcendence, their reality or material fullness (*Fülle*), and all admit of a meaning to potency and act. This meaning, however, cannot be investigated in a purely formal manner as act and potency concerns the *content* of being. This is why Stein's analysis of potency and act must take the form of a presentation of the analogy of being, of act and potency as bearing on spirit, nature and their presupposition in absolute being. The formal ontology of potency and act cannot be investigated in isolation, and thus the transcendental investigation of knowledge (of what these terms *mean*) leads to an investigation of reality in its basic articulations (of what these terms *refer to*).[35]

In *Potency and Act* Stein works with several of her characteristic ideas: the ontological status of ideal or essential being, knowledge of the individual, in particular of the human individual, the nature of matter, the core of the person, evolution and life. The contrasting of the scholastic and the phenomenological approach already yields significant results. On the one hand the phenomenologically experienced unity of the I makes Aquinas' understanding of the immateriality of the soul show up as being in contrast with the idea that what individuates everything, and thus also the soul, should be matter. On the other hand the incontrovertible being of the I, as underlined by Husserl, makes it impossible to avoid the ontological investigation (of the *being* of the I) to which Aquinas' contributes.

Finite and Eternal Being

The novice mistress and sub-prior at St Maria *des Friedens*, Sr Teresia Renata, somewhat unexpectedly, encouraged Stein to finish *Potency and Act* for publication, having a high regard for Stein's abilities and for what she must have seen as Stein's special mission. As Stein undertook this work, her external circumstances had changed: she no longer was under an economic

35   PA, III, §4.

obligation to teach or to pursue a career, time was regularly given to writing, and the quiet disengagement from the world left her room to think and study within the safe, but austere, haven of a religious community, hidden in a world marked by terror and violence.

Finite and Eternal Being takes, compared to *Potency and Act*, a different direction already in the first chapter, where Stein reflects on the possibility of (or indeed the necessity for) a Christian philosophy to account for the structure of reality. Maritain had claimed for moral philosophy the need to be supported by Christian principles for the moral philosopher to accede to moral truth, not only because grace would strengthen his intellectual powers, but because Christian doctrine underpins it (the dignity and equality of all human beings as children of God, love as their vocation). Stein claims this support is needed for philosophy as such – not only for anthropology, but also for ontology, as indeed the revelation in the Word of God is of a God that *wants* relation and *is* relation, in which all relations find their ultimate meaning as the meaning of being. The idea that philosophy could achieve its goal (*perfectum opus rationis*) without recourse to Revelation was still – if only implicitly – affirmed in *Potency and Act*. Now it is explicitly denied: philosophy achieves its purpose through theology, but not *as* theology.

The consideration of formal ontology is now replaced by a (phenomenological) analysis of essence and essentiality as forms of essential being.[36] *Form* along with *matter* now seems secondary compared to essence to Stein (and with form and matter the distinction between formal and material ontology).[37] A close discussion of Aristotle has the purpose of determining

---

36 Stein conducts this inquiry in dialogue with Jean Hering, 'Bemerkungen über das Wesen, die Wesenheit und die Idee'.

37 The distinction between form and content, empty form and fulfilment or 'filling' now moves to the forefront to account for the family likenesses of things. Form and content are distinct through the type of understanding (*Anschauung*) we can have of them: The content when contemplated allows the spirit to come to rest in the ultimate essentialities, the abstracted form refers beyond itself because of its emptiness and hence does not allow the spirit to rest in the same way. EES V, § 2, p. 242. This, however, does not cancel the idea of formal ontology but rather completes

the relationship between his concept of essence (*to ti en einai*) and the phenomenological one. In the course of this investigation the concepts of substance and form are equally discussed to determine their relevance for the phenomenological concept of essence previously clarified, and the ideas of matter, mass and material (*Stoff*) are compared, so as to clarify the Aristotelian concept of matter on the one hand and proceed towards an adequate understanding of concreteness and of the bearer (*hypostasis*, *Träger*) of the being and its essence on the other.

Having discussed essence in relation to concreteness, Stein turns in chapter V towards being as such, i.e. towards the transcendentals: the being something, one, true, good and beautiful of everything. The divisions of being into spirit, nature and infinite being has revealed all being, transcendent and immanent, as standing in a potential and/or real relationship with spirit (everything stands in a relationship with the divine spirit). This has opened up the possibility of everything being true and good, i.e. of everything being known and being appreciated for what it is, i.e. in a certain respect: not everything is good for everything else. Knowledge, insofar as it is a relationship to the object, 'helps to build up the *what* of knowledge and is the condition of its reality'.[38] It belongs to all being to be open to be the object of such knowledge: that is what is meant by characterising truth as a transcendental. 'Being is (even if its full meaning is not exhausted by this) being revealed to the spirit'.[39]

The meaning of being treated in chapter VI relies on this division internal to being between nature and spirit, which allows being a meaning, i.e. a 'being for', a 'being revealed to'. This meaning amounts to being as such having a definite relationship with a certain type of being, namely spirit, and thus it amounts to a relationship internal to being, which is itself intelligible, like being, and intelligible because it *is*.

---

it as metaphysics: 'Alles Seiende ist Fülle in einer Form. Die Formen des Seienden herauszustellen ist die Aufgabe der Wissenschaft, die Husserl als *'formale Ontologie'* bezeichnet hat.' Ibid., p. 243.

38   EES, V,§ 10, p. 254. My transl.
39   Ibid., p. 258. My transl.

What is common to the meaning of (all finite) being (where essence and being differ) is that it is the:

> *unfolding of a meaning; essential being is timeless unfolding beyond the difference between potency and act; real being is unfolding out of an essential form, from potency to act, in time and space; the being of thought is unfolding in several senses* [...].[40]

Apart from unfolding, being also is, in accordance with its transcendental characteristics, one, true, good, beautiful and something, something with content (*erfülltes*). 'We *mean* this complete fullness when we talk of "being". But a finite spirit cannot comprehend this fullness fully. It is the infinite task of insight.'[41]

The contrast between formal and material ontology – between form and content as understood by Husserl[42] – is thus replaced by one of ideal and real being, while essence moves to the foreground to replace form and matter as basic concepts. The meaning of being is approached as the happening and valuing of the mutual relations between the different kinds of being and each individual being. This ascent to the meaning of being, as the subtitle indicates, no longer proceeds by penetrating into the meaning of act and potency (as in *Potency and Act*), but by penetrating experience to the meaning of being itself. The rewriting of *Potency and Act* made Stein accomplish a shift in presuppositions: as the concepts of form and matter as structural features of the system of being were replaced, a new phenomenological ontology became possible, on a Christian foundation, in the *Logos*. The transcendental structure of knowledge now takes its place at the heart of ontology, opening up the distinction between nature and spirit and leaving room for an infinite spirit whose correspondence with being in truth is identical to itself and has revealed itself in Christ.

---

40   Ibid., VI, § 1, pp. 284–5. My transl. The corresponding passage is CWES IX, p. 331.
41   Ibid., p. 286: 'We mean this total fullness when we speak of 'being'. But a finite spirit is never able to apprehend this fullness in the unity of a fulfilling intuition. It is the infinite task of our knowing.' My transl. The corresponding passage is CWES IX, p. 332.
42   Edmund Husserl, *Logical Investigations,* transl. by J.N. Findlay (London–New York: Routledge, 2001).V, 2, § 14–15.

***

Insofar as the idea that matter is the principle of individuation is not essential to Thomism, one can call Stein's ontology Thomist or Thomistic. More importantly however, Stein's *Seinslehre* is an attempt to advance Christian philosophy in the tradition of the *philosophia perennis*, to which also Aquinas wanted to contribute. It may be more fruitful to see them both as parallel endeavours of the same species, instead of trying to place Stein's as a subspecies of the species to which Aquinas' philosophy belongs.

The fact that she is a Thomist and a phenomenologist (only) in so far as she is both, challenges us to cross categories established by major events in the history of ideas. This challenge was one she was aware of having a special vocation to meet, but also one which she considered the philosophy as such obliged to meet. To her, philosophy concerns *the things themselves*, and thus the history of ideas would have to be a discipline enabling discussion of these, as much as it is relying on it.

CHAPTER 10

Beginning to Read *Finite and Eternal Being*

Beginning to read Stein's *Finite and Eternal Being* is somewhat daunting, as one seems to remain at the level of beginning for quite some time. To assist that beginning, I shall here give an overview of the preoccupations that structure the work. As after a number of readings of the work I still consider myself a beginner, it may well be that some accents are misplaced and some essential issues are left unaddressed.[1]

We shall first characterise the tendencies implicit in Stein's work as a whole, since it is it as a whole, which comes to fruition in *Finite and Eternal Being* (1). Then we shall examine her claim that the investigation of the meaning of being must, for the believer, take account of Revelation, and thus be Christian philosophy (2). As the philosophy resulting can be characterised equally as phenomenology and metaphysics, an explanation of how these disciplines are related in the work is required. The difference between the two subjects can best be stated in relation to ontology: whereas phenomenology essentially includes a reference to formal ontology,

---

1   The work was planned to appear at Frankes Verlag in Stein's hometown Breslau (See R. Leuven and L. Gelber, 'Nachvort' in *Endliches und Ewiges Sein*, ESW, 1986 (first printing 1950), pp. 483–97, p. 483). Before then it was planned as part of the series 'Christliches denken' with Anton Pustet in Salzburg (Letter to Conrad-Martius, *Selbstbildness in Briefen* 1933–42 no. 483, 10 October 1936). But after having delayed the publication for four years, the project was given up due to the prohibition on the publication of books written by non-Arians. Negotiations were undertaken with a view to publication in America (the types were already set, amounting to one and a half tons of lead), but the project stranded on the relatively minor readership a work in German could expect to find in the States, despite the many refugees from the Holocaust. See Stephen Payne: 'Foreword to the ICS Publications Edition', FEB, pp. xiii–xxii; p. xv.

metaphysics includes both formal and material ontologies in a view of the whole. Thus we shall examine the relationship of phenomenology and formal ontology in (3), so as to be able to clarify the relationship between these and metaphysics in (4).

From Stein's early work in phenomenology (1915–20) through *Introduction to Philosophy* (1920–30) and *The Structure of the Human Person/What is the Human Being?* (1930), to culmination in *Finite and Eternal Being* (1936) and *Science of the Cross* (1942), an unfolding or maturing is to be observed, which sets the scene for understanding *Finite and Eternal Being* as a final or concluding statement. We shall endeavour to explain how *Finite and Eternal Being*, by the fact that we can characterise it in the manners proposed, achieves a unity aimed at by Stein from her earliest writings.

The tendencies implicit in Stein's work as a whole

Stein shows from her earliest writings exceptional awareness of how various types of sociality influence thought, i.e. how they provide the setting for the experiencing I. Thinking, for Stein, and as a consequence philosophy, is not a context-independent exercise: it not only reflects the social setting in which it occurs, it also depends on it. The choice of context that a philosopher makes is therefore one that will not only be reflected in her or his philosophy, but also one that will substantially contribute to the philosophy itself. This is something the thinker can count on, and indeed must reckon with: the context is the setting of the text she or he produces. Stein's choice of the context of the Catholic Church for her middle and later thought must be seen in this light, and we must expect that she chose that context because she considered her thinking best served by it. The best context is the one that allows for the deepest possible insight, but, given that a context is real and really maintained in a real community of real people with many different agendas, the same context may also constrain, just like any work environment is both enabling and constraining. Stein's engagement with the nature of Christian philosophy prolongs her desire to think with, and in, a context, and her reflection on the topic in the introduction to *Finite and Eternal Being* remains one of the most interesting accounts in the context of the 'Modernist Crisis'.[2]

As thought has its context provided by the community that sustains it, it likewise contributes to such a context. Hence Stein is aware of creating a climate for the reader and offers herself as someone who thinks the perspective of the reader is as important as that of the author. Stein is a 'with-thinker' by profound conviction, and as a consequence she is always relying on the reader to test what she says by personal insight; implying by this, both that it is possible to think 'with' another, and that the world-view proposed by an author is open to be tested by the life experience of people who engage with it. Neither could be taken quite for granted in the philosophical environment she came from; both reflect contributions Stein made to that context.

That Stein believes in 'with-thinking' as a phenomenologist allows her to compare thinkers in a manner that is both simple and highly reflective: because she presupposes that every thinker is attempting to express some aspect of things themselves, every kind of thought testifies to them, by being a perspective on them. The essence of things is *a priori* intuitable by anyone, but not all intuit in the same way. As perspectives may be compared to establish the partiality of each, understanding each perspective allows one to understand the things in question and assess their essence better.[3] This kind of comparison is the key to understand Stein's

---

2   EES, pp. 20–36. The present English translation of the work by Kurt Reinhart (CWES IX) needs to be read alongside this critical edition, which in contrast with the first Herder edition contains the two appendixes on Martin Heidegger and Teresa of Avila. FEB is currently being retranslated by Walter Redmond in its entirety and will appear with the appendixes in the CWES shortly.

3   The perspective of the early Heidegger, for example, is explained as an attempt to reduce the meaning of being to the meaning of the being of the human being, in a manner that actually allows for a very penetrating analysis of this being (in its fallen state). See Chapter 11.

attempt to bring together phenomenology and Thomism: insofar as they both are perspectives on things themselves, understanding the manner in which they relate to each other allows one to better grasp what each attempts to grasp and establish the relationship between the things thus grasped. What remains the focus of such a comparison, however, are the things themselves, upon which the perspective sheds light, and indeed of which the perspectives form part. The recourse to the perspectives of others is therefore constantly subordinated to the revelatory capacity of the perspectives as regards the things themselves. In this view the things are therefore *ipso facto* taken to admit of different perspectives on them, and therefore to be something intelligible *in themselves*, i.e. independently of individual perspectives, although not necessarily independent of any possible perspective. The engagement with the things themselves thus goes hand in hand, not only with an understanding of the workings of inter-subjectivity, but also with an understanding of the *a priori* nature of the *eidos*, the essence of things.

It is the importance of community (as a type of inter-subjectivity) for thought that makes Stein thematise that which makes us comparable and binds us together: the fact that we are human beings. This is why the question of the human person remains central to her thought right through her life. The question is important because it stands at the root of the openness to and of the world: it is the question that addresses the 'hub' around which the inter-subjective world revolves and which as a consequence provides us with the best starting-point for our interpretation of it.

The inter-subjective dimension of the world makes her philosophy feel fuller than the transcendental idealism of the later Husserl and his disciples, but it remains a fact that she thought she learnt the understanding of it from the early Husserl. The underlining of the inter-subjective dimension allows Stein keen awareness of the possibilities for social construction to either hamper or foster the development of the human being and person. This leads her to reflect on the state, where the human being is both central and exposed, and on the state's essentially problematic relationship with religion, which claims a privileged relationship with the values upon which the state relies.[4] Stein's phenomenology is thus one that allows for and incorporates social analysis to an extent that Husserl's does not: it therefore feels not only fuller, but also more practical than his does.

Apart from the centrality of the human person and the underlining of the inter-subjective context which will lead her to reflect on the nature of Christian philosophy, the pursuits of phenomenology and formal ontology were also inherited from Husserl. It is this foundation, together with the insight that an investigation of being as such cannot be accomplished at the level of formal ontology (since being is also a matter of content and thus of material ontology), that allows her to discuss Aristotle's and Aquinas' perspectives on 'the things themselves' without leaving the methodological starting-point of phenomenology.[5] It is this double foundation that allows her to study the meaning of being as the unfolding of being to and for itself in nature, spirit and absolute being, and thus treat of the 'whole' of being, which is the task of metaphysics.

Finite and Eternal Being is undoubtedly close to Scholastic philosophy, both in the manner in which its discussions are conducted, and in the subjects discussed. We may be able to call it a work of Scholastic philosophy if by that we understand the type of philosophy which asks for the ultimate reasons and the meaning of being in the tradition of the *philosophia perennis*. It is also, however, a work of phenomenology addressing the question of being, thus achieving the funnelling of classical and modern ways of thinking into one stream of thought. The insistence on the fact that these different strands of thought must ultimately address the same things allows us to see them as providing essentially compatible perspectives on these things.

It is also, however, this wide contextuality (relying on what Gadamer calls a 'fusion of horizons') of the work that makes it difficult to access for those bound by loyalty to *either* classical *or* modern ways of thinking, and

---

4   *State*, II.
5   This foundation is elaborated in PE and PPH, as discussed in Chapters 2–4. See my 'Study-guide to Edith Stein's *Philosophy of Psychology and the Humanities*' in *Yearbook of the Irish Philosophical Society*, 2004, pp. 40–76.

who regard these as incompatible. It is difficult for those loyal to classical and medieval philosophy because the vocabulary, the starting-point, the methodology and the things not taken for granted are unfamiliar. It is difficult for those loyal to a modern context because Christian teachings are deliberately drawn upon as indispensable for accomplishing the ascent to the meaning of being, which is the stated intent of the work. If it also presents an obstacle to those loyal to a modern context that Stein discusses concepts from the metaphysics of Aristotle and Aquinas in great detail (although in fact very critically), it should be remembered that others of the tradition do the same, in particular Heidegger, and that her discussions may be regarded as parallel to his.

Such a widening of the context or merging of horizons is possible to the extent that phenomenology is ultimately a quest for the meaning of being that acknowledges the subjective starting-point of modern philosophy. Stein thought that it was and that the purpose of the methodological bracketing of prejudicial and dogmatic ontological affirmations precisely was to enable the quest to succeed. The use of phenomenology to indefinitely postpone the fulfilling of the quest can only, in her estimation, be explained by ulterior motives and cannot in any way be understood to form part of the essence of phenomenology without rendering it an irrational endeavour.

Having characterised the general tenor of Stein's work, let us now look at the proposed three characterisations of the content of *Finite and Eternal Being* in detail and examine them in turn, reading the work as a concluding statement of the tendencies inherent in Stein's thought.

Christian philosophy

The Introduction to *Finite and Eternal Being* contains, as already mentioned, a section on the 'Meaning and Possibility of a "Christian Philosophy"' (§ 4). Here Stein justifies the taking account of Christian doctrine in the doing of philosophy and claims that so doing is what the believer will want to do, in so far as he recognises the insight of faith to be divinely inspired and reflecting things which, although obscure to the mind reaching out into 'the dark night of faith', are nevertheless understood to be higher and deeper than those accessible by the sole light of natural understanding. Stein claims it would in fact be unreasonable for the believer, i.e. for anyone accepting that the Revelation of God is available to us, not to take such revelation into account, given that what is implied in this belief is that God's superior wisdom has made itself accessible to us, like one human being reveals something of his inner life to another by opening himself up to him. Such Christian philosophy, relying on the testimony of others as regards the Other who is God, is relying on the testimony of the 'Christian community' for its context (like philosophy of natural science relies on the testimony of the community of scientists to provide its context). It also contributes to this context, like philosophy of science contributes to the scientific context, by making a theme of this testimony. In this sense Christian philosophy exemplifies a context-sensitive kind of philosophy, which, like other contexts, remains essentially open for anyone to test by his own lights, taking as hypotheses what the Christian (or the scientist) accepts as theses.

However, one might not be able to call this Christian philosophy, which takes account of Revelation, 'pure' philosophy, insofar as one understands pure philosophy to be a purely 'natural' science, i.e. a science relying on natural insight alone, as distinct from 'supernatural' insight. It is necessary to recall, however, that the idea of a distinction between 'natural' and 'supernatural' insight in the first place is of Christian origin and intends to describe the difference between what we can 'come up with' independently of Revelation, and what Revelation by itself contributes. The distinction should in other words make mere hypothetical sense to someone who does not believe there is such a thing as Revelation, and as such it would form part of the (Christian) context. It is 'the Thomistic stand-point,' however, (and here Stein refers specifically to Maritain) that pure philosophy does not involve the taking account of

Revelation.[6] To the Thomist, therefore, Stein's Christian philosophy would quite likely not be 'pure'. However, insofar as the task of philosophy is to penetrate into 'the ultimate meaning, to being itself, to the constitution of beings as such',[7] then one cannot afford, according to Stein, to disregard the light Revelation sheds on these matters, as it indeed does shed significant light on them. Stein reminds us that the Church Fathers understood Christianity *as* (their) philosophy precisely because they regarded it to substantially further this central aim of philosophy. To them, the purity of philosophy depends on its relationship with truth, not on whether or not it takes Revelation into account.

In the same way as Maritain distinguishes between the 'nature' and 'state' of philosophy, and thinks that the Christian state of philosophy allows it a better grasp of the final end of the human being and therefore of moral philosophy, so Stein thinks that the Christian state of philosophy – not only relying on the grace pertaining to individuals or on the philosophical advances resulting from the clarification of theological matters, but directly on the states of affairs 'known' by the light of faith (Creation, the Fall, Redemption and the End) – allows it to grasp the meaning of being better than if it renounced the guidance of the light of faith.[8] Still more radically put: if philosophy is the science of the ultimate, whose goal is final clarity and the final understanding of the states of affairs that obtain, it cannot dispense with the light of faith insofar as faith also claims to know something about these ultimate states of affairs.[9] For the non-believer, Stein claims, it must be quite intelligible that the believer thinks in this way, and indeed that it is part of the way his faith has importance for him. The non-believer should thus be able to replace the theses which the believer accepts by faith with hypotheses that could be accepted if one

6   EES, I, § 4, p. 20 note 2.
7   Ibid., p. 27.
8   Ibid., p. 30.
9   Ibid., p. 27.

believed. In this way the perspective of the Christian philosopher is open to the non-believer as context dependent, in the same way as any other context-dependent perspective is.

This science of the ultimate, philosophy as the '*perfectum opus rationis*', is essentially incomplete, because it is of the ultimate and because the human mind is finite not only in relation to it, but also in its ability to take other perspectives into account. The essential incompleteness of philosophy makes it open to being and to further developments in other sciences, including that of theology. Stein saw this essential openness of philosophy as regards the perspectives of others already in *Philosophy of Psychology and the Humanities*: The depth of the world as comprehended by the very many subjects, past, present and future, to whom the I can relate also by understanding, reflects the depth of the wisdom that must be God's, infinite, all-present and all-embracing. *The Structure of the Human Person*, Stein's philosophical anthropology, underlines the openness in relation to the ultimate, in that it has its complementary counterpart in the collection of dogmatic declarations assembled in *What is the Human Being?* These dogmatic declarations shed light of a kind that leaves the reader impressed by the understanding of the human being available from them and with the awareness of how profoundly they must have shaped Christian and European thought.

By acknowledging its context-dependence, debt to Revelation and consequent essential openness, Christian philosophy may contribute to the awareness of the openness of any context into which it is taken up. As such it is achieved in community by individuals attracted to or affected by the light of Christ. *Finite and Eternal Being* is Christian philosophy in this sense: compared to Maritain's Thomism, it is both more open to a diversity of perspectives, and more substantially Christian in that it allows for Redemption to concern the meaning of being.

Phenomenology and formal ontology

Finite and Eternal Being is not only Christian philosophy. It is also phenomenology and indeed represents a concluding stage of Stein's engagement with this discipline. Phenomenology, however, also comports ontology, in particular formal ontology.

To Stein, as to all the early phenomenologists, including Husserl, the most important purpose of phenomenology was to found the sciences by clarifying their objects. To this end eidetic and constitutional analyses had to be deployed to establish formal and material ontologies, upon which the sciences could rest: the material ontologies investigating the objects of the particular sciences (e.g. chemical composition, physical forces, life) grouped under regional ontologies investigating the higher order objects (e.g. nature, spirit). The topmost layer was to be constituted by formal ontology, which was to investigate the empty forms of something (*Etwas*) or of being as such.

Eidetic analysis, the investigation of the essences in terms of which we make sense of our experience, is a type of analysis that does not pronounce judgement about whether phenomena *in fact* reflect an existing reality, but rather turn attention to the structure of what is experienced and to what must pertain to this experienced something for an experience to be of it (e.g. what must pertain to a moth for my experience of it to be an experience of a moth or what must pertain to perception for my experience to be a perception). Eidetic analysis is thus concerned with the essential being of things and does not compromise the phenomenological method by addressing things outside the phenomenological reduction. It is thus to be expected that formal ontology concerns essential being.

Hans Rainer Sepp characterises in his foreword to *Potency and Act*, the forerunner of *Finite and Eternal Being*, the difference between Husserl's and Stein's understanding of the relationship between transcendental phenomenology and formal ontology in the following way:

> Stein requires, like Husserl, a 'starting-point' [... but ...] for Stein the fact of the activity of the subject is not an occasion to suspend the question of the being of this immanent

act [... It is rather so that ...] this act itself, its actuality, discloses in its temporality, i.e. in its continual passing from potentiality to actuality, *ex negativo* the 'idea of pure being', which escapes temporality [...] If Husserl takes the starting-point to clear the absolute immanent sphere of transcendental subjectivity, so Stein takes the constituting function of subjectivity as an occasion to show that subjectivity needs and refers to something that it is itself not. That [subjectivity] is constituting – and that means 'temporalising' time and 'decaying' subjectivity – refers it to something non-temporal; that it constantly constitutes something refers it to something that does not coincide with its own immanent being. Thus Stein is brought to affirm a sphere of pure being (a transcendent sphere in a second sense) which must be distinguished from both the immanent sphere and the sphere of transcendence announced in the former as distinct. The discipline which attempts to circumscribe the meaning of being in all [of these] spheres is that of Formal Ontology.

Thus is revealed that Formal Ontology is not, for Stein, as it is for Husserl, subordinated to transcendental phenomenology, but has a reciprocal relationship with it. Formal Ontology is for Stein referred to transcendental phenomenology, insofar as this latter is not only treating of the relationship between the immanent and the transcendent spheres, but also must question the constitution of the entities of Formal Ontology. Transcendental Philosophy is referred in the opposite direction to Formal Ontology, not only because it is the task of the latter to determine the meaning of immanence in conjunction with the material ontologies, but because it falls to it to clarify in a general way the fundamental ontological concepts.[10]

The reciprocal relationship between formal ontology and transcendental phenomenology (between the analysis of essence and the analysis of how things are constituted for us within consciousness) is one Stein probably took to be constitutive to phenomenology, so that she would regard it as impossible to subordinate one discipline to another in the way Sepp here claims that Husserl did. For the phenomenological reduction to yield a field of meaning to be investigated by transcendental phenomenology there must be a field of meaning that can be investigated. The analysis of this meaning calls for a related discipline that clarifies the meanings possible, investigates how they relate to one another and perhaps condition one another. This is formal ontology.

10 Hans Rainer Sepp, 'Einführung des Bearbeiters' in PA, ESW 18, p. XXIV–V; ESGA 10, p. XXIII–XXIV; translated in CWES 11, p. xxx–xxxi (but this translation is my own).

Stein's use of the phenomenological starting-point, i.e. of the possibility to reduce experience to how it is experienced or to subjective experience (mediated by inter-subjective experience), is thus methodological, and its purpose is to achieve final clarity about the ultimate things, the things themselves. The starting-point forms the platform for showing that the subject has experience of something which transcends the temporal existence it recognises as its own – the suspension over the swords-edge of the *now*. These are the units of experience, which it experiences as lasting in time and indeed as revelatory of things, like 'joy as such', the being of which is not temporal at all. Essences, as experienced by the subject understanding its experience as intelligible because of them, are not essentially temporal as the experience of the subject is; they don't rely on time for their being.

Metaphysics and material ontology

However, being as such cannot be reduced to essential being. There is also real being, i.e. being which we experience *a posteriori*, as a matter of fact. It is because of it that we know *of* chemical composition, physical forces and life from experience, not merely *what* these are. Experience as we know it is not only *a priori*. If, therefore, we want to investigate the meaning of being as Stein does in *Finite and Eternal Being*, we cannot remain at the level of essential being only. We must investigate that which essential and real being have in common as only that can claim to be being as such. Metaphysics must thus involve material ontology, all the concrete objects that form part of our experience, and which we experience as real.

Inter-subjective experience also points us in the direction of things that are experienced as having an essence as well as being factually present: things must not only be intelligible and have essence for them to be possible objects of inter-subjective experience, they must also be actually there, not merely potentially there, for them to be identifiable by several subjects as present. Formal ontology does not deal with the content of being, and for some being (namely real or actual being) content (*Fülle*, the difference between potential and actual) is of the essence. Stein had to write *Potency and Act* to provide her with this insight, but she did not need to publish it because the insight made her understand the phenomenological starting point in a new manner, in such a way as to be able to write *Finite and Eternal Being*.

That there is a methodological starting-point, and that this is in the subject who has 'indubitable' experience of its experience as experienced and therefore has a laboratory in which concepts can be clarified, tested and compared, is something Stein insists on also in *Finite and Eternal Being*. The starting point now, however, is a starting point *for* the quest for the meaning of being, and it is one that is had in the being of the I itself.

The meaning of being is thus all of the following:

- that being is articulated in transcendent, subjective and pure being;
- that being is refracted for the spirit in nature, spirit and absolute being;
- that this articulation and this refraction is the image of the Trinity in its Creation;
- that all this can be known with reference to essential being that structures the mind as such and inhabits the divine mind as its ideas; and
- that being nevertheless cannot be reduced to essential being.

The meaning of being is being in its fullness, all of being, the whole, which properly speaking is the object of metaphysics.

***

The '*perfectus opus rationis*' of Christian philosophy must not only proceed methodically and therefore adopt the best method available (which in Stein's view is phenomenology). It must also stay faithful to the entirety of what it asks even if it means going beyond what the method seems capable of accommodating.

This meaning of being is investigated equally and simultaneously by the three disciplines that essentially characterise *Finite and Eternal Being*: Christian Philosophy, Phenomenology and Metaphysics. Stein achieved this ascent to the meaning of being by engaging with Husserl and Aquinas alike, showing that the science of philosophy need be neither exclusively allied to ancient or modern philosophy. Philosophy thus can be universally accessible. To show this was the ambition to which her engagement with philosophy pointed from her earliest career onwards.

CHAPTER 11

Heidegger and the Meaning of Being

Appended to Stein's 'spiritual testament' *Finite and Eternal Being. An Attempt at an Ascent to the Meaning of Being* we find a long essay entitled: *Martin Heidegger's Existential Philosophy.*[1] A shorter essay on the *Castle of the Soul* by Theresa of Avila is also appended.[2]

---

1   As the new, complete translation of *Finite and Eternal Being* has not appeared yet, I refer to the page numbers of the German text (ESGA), although I quote from my own translation published in the *Maynooth Philosophical Papers*, 2007 (<http://eprints.nuim.ie/1005>). *Finite and Eternal Being* was written in the years 1935–6, just after Stein had finished her novitiate in the Cologne Carmel. It is an extensive revision of Stein's habilitation attempt *Potency and Act*, which was, when submitted in Freiburg in November 1931, read by, among others, Martin Heidegger. Also the Thomist Martin Honnecker red the manuscript, but did not think highly of it (Hugo Ott, op. cit.). Heidegger discussed the manuscript of *Potenz und Act* with Stein for 2 hours (Letter to Ingarden 151 (25 December 1931) and 152 (9 March 1932)). Heidegger and Honnecker both advised Stein that she would be acceptable for habilitation on previous work, but also that she should not proceed for political reasons. This attempt was her second, of which we have an extant written work (the first being *Beiträge*, ESGA 6). *Einführung in der Philosophie* (ESGA 8), which Lucy Gelber regarded as a third habilitation attempt for Breslau (ESW XIII) is more likely, as claimed by Wulf in her introduction to ESGA 8, to be the series of lectures held by Stein in Breslau, at which assisted among others Norbert Elias (Letters to Fritz Kaufmann (ESGA 2) 31–2, pp. 56–9). Although Stein herself talks about a revision, *Finite and Eternal Being* is in fact an entirely different work compared to *Potency and Act*. *Potency and Act* is a *Formalontologie* in the Husserlian sense and does not yet carry the large scale *Auseinandersetzung* with Aquinas and Aristotle, which makes up the middle part of *Finite and Eternal Being*.

2   Both of these were left out in the first edition of Stein's works by Herder, *Edith Steins Werke* (ESW). The new critical edition *Edith Stein Gesamtausgabe* (ESGA) has amended this, and the English translation is catching up: the Heidegger-appendix

An appendix is always an awkward thing to analyse as its status remains somewhat unclear. It was deemed important enough to be appended to the main work by the author, but it was not directly included in it. It is clear from a letter to Conrad-Martius that the appendices were written after the main work was completed.[3] However, to judge from the level of importance the other appendix has for the understanding of Stein's thought, this one too should give insight into an important aspect of it. The appendix on Theresa of Avila's *Interior Castle* gives an analysis of the soul's experience of its own depths in the context of mystical life, which confirms Stein's early phenomenological analyses. If the Heidegger appendix gives us something of equal importance, what is it?

In the following we shall discuss the reasons Stein had to write about Heidegger (1). Then we shall turn to Stein's discussion of Heidegger's project (2). We shall finally outline Stein's and Heidegger's alternative phenomenological inheritance and their relationship to the meaning of being (3).

Why did Stein write about Heidegger?

The appendix provides a key to *Finite and Eternal Being*, which can be read, because of it, as a response to Heidegger's *Being and Time*.[4] Such a reading on its own, however, would not do the work justice, since its

is due to be included in a new translation of *Finite and Eternal Being* by Walter Redmond to appear in CWES.

3   Letter to Hedwig Conrad-Martius, 20 August 1936, ESGA 3, letter 473, p. 221; CWES 5, p. 233, letter 224.

4   Other investigations of the relationship between Stein and Heidegger includes: John Nota, 'Edith Stein and Martin Heidegger', in Edith Stein Symposium, *Carmelite Studies* 4, ed. John Sullivan (Washington D.C.: ICS Publications, 1987) pp. 50–73 (a German version is found in *Denken in Dialog: zur Philosophie Edith Steins,* ed. Waltraud Herbstrith (Tübingen: Attempto Verlag, 1991) pp. 93–117); Antonio Calcagno, 'Die Fülle oder das Nichts? Edith Stein and Martin Heidegger on the

investigation of the meaning of being points to the meaning of being itself for its meaning. Reading the work as a reply to Heidegger must remain an afterthought, since the positive content of the work does not directly concern Heidegger's work. When the thought nevertheless occurs, it is because *Finite and Eternal Being* answers the same question concerning the meaning of being as *Being and Time* does, but in contrast with the latter retains a focus on being as such and not only on the human being in its ascent to the meaning of being.

Stein had met Heidegger, first at the Husserls' in Freiburg, and later at several occasions while she was working as Husserl's assistant. She had found him charming, but had also noticed that his writings contained 'unmistakable digs at phenomenology'.[5] She understood Heidegger to take the phenomenological inheritance in a direction that led away from Husserl's original insights, and warily observed Husserl placing his full trust in Heidegger.[6] As she associated herself with Husserl's vision for

---

Question of Being' in *American Catholic Philosophical Quarterly*, Vol. LXXIV, No. 2 (revised for Antonio Calcagno, *The Philosophy of Edith Stein* (Duquesne University Press: Pittsburgh, 2007), which is the edition we have used and refer to); Hugo Ott, 'Edith Stein und Freiburg', in *Studien zur Philosophie von Edith Stein* (Freiburg – Munich: Verlag Karl Alber, 1993) pp. 107–45 also gives an account of Stein's and Heidegger's interactions in the early Freiburger years; Lidia Ripamonti, 'Being Thrown or Being held in Existence? The opposite Approaches to Finitude of Edith Stein and Martin Heidegger', in *Yearbook of the Irish Philosophical Society* 2008, ed. Fiachra Long, pp. 71–83. Marianne Sawicki's *Body Text and Science* (Kluwer: Dordrecht, 1997) treats of Heidegger's publication of Husserl's *Time Consciousness* (which Stein edited), but not of Stein's Heidegger critique, which belongs to the writings of the later Stein. Alisdair MacIntyre is right in contrasting Heidegger's attitude to the relevance of philosophy for the living of ordinary life with Stein's (*Edith Stein. A Philosophical Prologue 1913–1922* (New York – Toronto – Oxford: Rowman and Littlefield Publishers, 2006) pp. 5–6).

5   Life, p. 409 – she was referring in particular to Heidegger's inaugural lecture: *What is Metaphysics?*

6   Letter to Ingarden 15 October 1921: 'Heidegger geniesst Husserls absolutes Vertrauen und benutzt es, um die Studentenschaft, auf die er starkeren Einfluss hat als Husserl selbst, in einer Richtung zu führen, die von Husserl ziemlich weit abliegt. Ausser dem guten Meister weiss das jedermann.' ESGA 4, letter 78, pp. 143–4.

phenomenology as the foundation for future collaboration in philosophy, she saw Heidegger's 'digs' as an attack on what she had found most valuable in phenomenology.[7] Writing on Heidegger was an opportunity to speak for phenomenology against the direction in which he took it. It was also an opportunity to address the question of being as also Hedwig Conrad-Martius and Roman Ingarden had done.[8]

Heidegger's turn towards being or towards the meaning of being was a turn towards 'Dasein' *as* the meaning of being, in prolongation of Husserl's transcendental idealism. To Stein, the subordination of eidetics to transcendental phenomenology in Husserl's later philosophy, in contrast, constituted a problem. She saw the essential structures and the consequent foundation of a science of phenomenology as necessary for the Cartesian starting-point to be of any consequence and understood the

7   Letter to Ingarden 9 October 1926: 'Aber – nun kommt das wirklich Tragische an der Sache – dieses Ganze [of Husserl's thought] lebt wohl in ihm und er kann in guten Stunden davon sprechen, doch ich bezwifle, dass er es je zu Papier, geschweige denn in den Druck bringen wird, und er hat schlechterdings keinen Schüler, der ganz in seinem Sinne arbeitet. Wenn er mal emeritiert wird, dann wird er vermutlich selbst Heidegger als Nachfolger vorschlagen, und der geht eigene Wege.' ESGA 4, letter 100, pp. 171–2.
8   Hedwig Conrad-Martius, *Zur ontologie und Erscheinungslehre der realen Aussenwelt. Verbunden mit einer Kritik positivistischer Theorien*, in *Jahrbuch für Philosophie und Phanomenologische Forschung* 3 (1916), pp. 345–542; *Metaphysische Gespräche* (Halle: 1921); *Realontologie* in *Jahrbuch für Philosophie und Phänomenologische Forschung*, 6 (1923) pp. 159–333; Roman Ingarden, *Essentiale Fragen. Ein Beitrag zum Wesensproblem*, in *Jahrbuch für Philosophie und Phanomenologishe Forschung*, 5, 1925, p. 125 ff. Stein says in a letter to Ingarden 2 October 1927: 'Dass man auf dem Wege der Konstitutions-Probleme (die ich gewiss nicht unterschätze) zum Idealismus geführt werden müsse oder könne, glaube ich nicht. Es scheint mir, dass diese Frage überhaupt nicht auf philosophischem Wege entscheidbar ist, sondern immer schon entschieden ist, wenn jemand anfängt zu philosophieren. Und weil hier eine letzte persönliche Einstellung mitspricht, ist es auch bei Husserl verständlich, dass dieser Punkt für ihn indiskutabel ist.' (ESGA 4, letter 111, p. 185). *Einführung* also leaves the question undecided, but does not regard it as impossible for this reason to engage in formal ontology ((I, c), 7, pp. 75–9).

possibilities for future research into axiology and the normative sciences to rely on this. The investigation of essences took up a prominent place in Husserl's early philosophy: formal ontology was understood to formally determine the regions of the various regional ontologies, in the same way as the science of essence (*Wesenswissenshaft*) was a necessary presupposition for the sciences of reality (*Tatsachenwissenschaften*). That formal ontology should rely on the constituting function of the transcendental ego for the constitution of the formality it obeyed was clear to Stein in the sense that the constituting function is required in order to identify this formality. That this formality, however, should rely on the constituting function of the transcendental ego in order to be what it is *in itself* could be possible only if this ego was infinite. If conceived as temporal, the idea was parallel to Heidegger's reduction of being to Dasein, and of being to time. Discussing the meaning of being – finite and eternal being – would allow one to clarify this and to focus on being and its meaning without reducing it to the human being.

Stein's discussion of Heidegger's project

Stein's essay is divided into four sections, each concerned with one of Heidegger's (until then) published works: *Being and Time, Kant and the Problem of Metaphysics, The Essence of Reasons* and *What is Metaphysics?* About two thirds is taken up with an analysis of *Being and Time*, again simply divided into an 'Outline of the Argument' and an 'Evaluation'. The latter part of this critique addresses three questions: 'What is Dasein?', 'Is the Analysis of Dasein Accurate?' and 'Is it sufficient for adequately addressing the Question of the Meaning of Being?'. The remainder of the analysis of Heidegger's work is concerned with testing whether the attempt at carrying through the threefold reduction outlined below is continued on from *Being and Time*.

Stein initially characterises Heidegger's investigations as 'often truly enlightening'[9] and as accurate 'in a certain sense' – 'in the sense namely that [they] reveal something of the basic constitution of the human being, and sketches a certain way of being human with great clarity.' She says she knows 'of no better expression for this way of being, which he calls Dasein and understands to pertain to all human beings, than *unredeemed being*.'[10] It is unredeemed in both of its two different modes of 'everyday' and 'authentic' being, and although she describes Heidegger's description of the alternation between these modes as 'masterly,'[11] she also regards it as flawed: 'the human way of being as such is caricatured despite its being elucidated in its ultimate depths.'[12]

She points to Heidegger's omission of any references to an I, subject, soul or person as particularly critical. It results from his attempt to go beyond the 'what' of the human being, but the lack of identification of important elements of the human being inevitably leads to an inexcusable confusion of ontology with anthropology, and of existence with *my* existence.

Stein understands Heidegger's project as an attempt to accomplish three impossible reductions: (a) reduction of the meaning of being to the human being; (b) reduction of the human being to its finitude and (c) the reduction of being to time.

9   EES, HA, *Sein und Zeit,* p. 445.
10   EES, HA, 2, 'Is the Analysis of Dasein Accurate?', p. 480.
11   EES, HA, 2, 'Is the Analysis of Dasein Accurate?' p. 465.
12   The quotation on p. 480 continues: 'Unredeemed is both its deteriorated everyday being, and that which he holds to be its authentic being. The first is the flight from authentic being, the avoiding of the question: "being or not being". The second is the decision for non-being against being, the turning down of true, authentic being.' EES, HA, 2. 'Is the Analysis of Dasein Accurate?'

The attempt to reduce the meaning of being to the human being

Heidegger starts as Aristotle did, by asking for the meaning of being.[13] Yet, instead of concentrating on the meaning of being, he enumerates the *conditions* for asking for the meaning of being. The condition upon which he focuses in particular is the being for which its own being is in question – 'Dasein' – literally 'existence', but which it can hardly be doubted that Heidegger employs to refer to the human being. He does that 'without opposing the being, as "that which is", with being itself',[14] and this enables him to claim for the human being two things which are generally reserved for God: 'the identity of essence and being', and that it is that 'from which alone information about the meaning of being is to be hoped for'.[15] And yet 'the human being does not simply mean being, but a particular way of being, in contrast with which there are others: the present-at-hand and the ready-to-hand ...'[16] and also the *being* of Dasein.

The identification of Dasein with the source of the meaningfulness of being[17] as well as with a particular kind of being among others accomplishes

---

13 Aristotle: *Metaphysics* V, 7; VI, 2; VII, 1.

14 EES, HA, 1. 'What is Dasein?' p. 463.

15 Ibid.

16 'Heidegger justifies his taking his point of departure in the analysis of Dasein with the fact that one can only ask a being for the meaning of being, to whose meaning an understanding of being belongs. And as Dasein not only has understanding for its own being, but also for other beings, one must start with an analysis of Dasein. But does not the opposite follow from this reasoning? Because the human being understands not only its own being but also other beings, it is not referred to its own being as the only possible way to the meaning of being. Certainly the self-understanding of being can be laid bare in its root and critical reservations be encountered from the start. But the possibility of taking a point of departure in either the being of things or primary being always persists.' (EES, HA, III. 'Is the Analysis of Dasein a Sufficient Foundation for Addressing the Question of the Meaning of Being Appropriately?').

17 'Thus transcendence is brought to the centre of the investigation: as metaphysics – the questioning p. 481; of being – lies in human nature, the foundation of metaphysics

the assimilation of Dasein's inability to be defined with being's inability
to be put in any genus. That the two kinds of being opposed to Dasein –
being present-at-hand and being ready-to-hand – are understood to be
dependent in their being on Dasein from whom they hold their relevance,
situates Dasein on a par with being simply. But that Dasein is simultaneously understood as a *kind* of being is underlined by the fact that Heidegger
often talks about the *being* of Dasein, distinguishing it from Dasein itself.[18]
It is this being (simultaneously a kind of being and being simply) which
has determinations (existentials). They must therefore on the one hand
remain very abstract in order to fit the dimensions of being in general and
on the other be disconnected from the human reality of body and soul,
the limitations of which they nevertheless reflect.

The attempt to reduce the human being to its finitude

Stein objects not only to Heidegger's reduction of the meaning of being
to the human being, but also to the human being being reduced to its
finitude. Although Stein conceives of experience as laid out in the 'now'
of time – deploying itself in past, present and future – she insists that
experience is experience of *something* and that the human kind of experiencing is also *something* which we can and do identify by constituting
it. Heidegger's rejection of engaging with *what* Dasein is leads him to
understand the constituting function experiencing itself as constituting
in time as the ultimate source of the meaning of being, and as the essence

---

must disclose in the constitution of the being of human beings that which is the
basis for their understanding of being. Fundamental ontology is therefore analysis
of Dasein and especially of its transcendence.' (EES, HA, 'Kant and the Problem of
Metaphysics', p. 485).

18   Dasein hence, 'sometimes designates human beings (referred to as "whom" or "self"),
sometimes the being of human beings (in which case the expression "the being of
Dasein" is used).' (EES, HA 1. 'What is Dasein?' p. 465).

of the human being (Dasein).[19] But for 'Dasein' to adequately disclose the meaning of being we must have an understanding of the whole of it, and this we are supposed to have in death.[20] Death, in Heidegger's understanding, is the end of Dasein, in such a manner, however, that it leaves undecided whether there is a life after death. But how can death be the end of Dasein if we cannot be sure that death is the end of Dasein? And how can death provide us with a perspective that enables us to grasp Dasein in its entirety because it is the end of Dasein, if it is not certain that it is the end of Dasein? If it is not sure that death is the end of Dasein, we are still lacking a feature that will enable us to understand Dasein in its entirety and hence an element of the meaning of Dasein, which makes it sufficient for understanding the meaning of being. Death, in other words, or finitude, cannot be the whole, or the end, of Dasein, nor can it be the meaning of being, if Dasein *might* continue to exist or might indeed exist as finalised by something else than death.

Other features of Dasein's finitude do not serve us any better to understand it as a whole. Authentic Dasein, marked by resoluteness and concern, understands its own possibilities, and throws itself forth to meet

19   She quotes him saying in the Kant-book: "'Time is pure intuition only in that it spontaneously performs the aspect of succession and, as an act both receptive and formative, pro-poses this aspect as such to itself. This pure intuition solicits itself by that which it intuits (forms) [...] Time is, by nature, pure affection of itself.' [...] "Time is not an active affection concerned with the ready-to-hand self; as pure, it forms the essence of all auto-solicitation. Therefore, if the power of being solicited as a self belongs to the essence of the finite subject, time as pure self-affection forms the essential structure of subjectivity [...] as pure self-affection, it originally forms finite selfhood in such a way that the self can become self-consciousness." "Pure self-affection provides the transcendental ground-structure of the finite self as such." (EES, HA, 'Kant and the Problem of Metaphysics', p. 486). Note here Heidegger's use of the term 'essence', which testifies to the fact that although he attempts to think without the 'what' and without essence, he still has to use these ideas to make intelligible what he intends to do.

20   EES, HA, 2. 'Dasein and Temporality' p. 452.

the demands of the situation and the moment.[21] But although this marks
a relative independence, the momentary existence of Dasein depends on
something beyond it: 'In the moment ... something meets us that perhaps no
other moment will offer. To "bring it out", i.e. to take it up completely into
one's own being, we must "open" ourselves to it and "hand ourselves over"
to it.'[22] But that means that it comes with *something* for which we must be
open, and that it comes to *something* that can be actualised or diminished
by it. Hence the moment, inseparable from the concern present in it, is,
rather than a manifestation of Dasein's wholeness in finitude, a sign of the
human being's openness to other kinds of being and in particular to the
eternal fullness of being to which it can abandon itself in the present. Far
from being the meaning of being, finitude is a characteristic of the human
being experiencing itself as open to the eternal meaning of being.[23] Thus
finite beings and finitude cannot be understood in themselves without
reference to eternal being, just as constitution is unintelligible without
that which is being constituted. Heidegger's attempt to reduce the human
being to its finitude is intelligible only as an impossible attempt to derive
what is constituted from constitution itself.

21   'How should we understand this, if not in the sense of the realisation of an essence
      or a specificity, which is given with being human (i.e. with which one is thrown
      into Dasein), that however, for its development needs free co-operation and hence
      is entrusted to one?' (EES, HA, 2. 'Is the Analysis of Dasein Accurate?' p. 477).
22   EES, HA, II. 'Is the Analysis of Dasein Accurate?', p. 477.
23   'It is clear, then, that the entire understanding of time given in *Being and Time* needs
      to be revised. Temporality, with its three "ekstases" and its extention, must have its
      meaning clarified as the way in which the finite gains participation in the eternal. The
      significance of the *future*, so strongly emphasised by Heidegger, must be explained in
      two ways. First as Heidegger does – as the *care* for its preservation stemming from
      understanding the flux and nothingness of one's own being; secondly as a direction
      towards a *fulfilment yet to come*, a transition from the dispersion of temporal being to
      the gathering of authentic, simple, eternity filled being. Moreover, the *present* must
      be seen as the *way of being of fulfilment*, which – like a flash of eternal light – opens
      up the understanding to being's fulfilment, as the *past* is the way of being that gives
      an impression of *durability* in the flux of our being.' EES, HA, II. 'Is the Analysis of
      Dasein Accurate?', p. 480.

The reduction of being to time

Heidegger's attempt to reduce the meaning of being to the constituting function of Dasein reveals his desire to identify what lies before the 'what', but it also entails that being as such is conceived according to the mode of being it has in the human being: being that is in time. To Stein it is significant that Heidegger never actually wrote the last section of *Being and Time*, which should have accomplished the reduction of being to time, but nevertheless refers to it in several places as an aspiration to which the work as a whole tends. Some attempt to finish the project (upon which the rest depends) can be found in *Kant and the Problem of Metaphysics*.[24] She interprets Heidegger to say: 'The human being must, in so far as it is, be able to *let be*, and for this it must "have already projected that which he encounters as a being." Existence (i.e. the human way of being) "is in itself *finitude* and, as such, is *only possible on the basis of the comprehension of being. There is and must be such as being only where finitude has become existent.*" In so far, however, as Heidegger is attempting to derive being from finitude without it either being or authentically becoming a 'what', he must understand nothing to be prior and original to being. He has in fact a tendency to go all the way and identify the being of Dasein with the nothingness it experiences in its finite being.[25] Not only does he thus identify the being of Dasein with nothingness, but also the being whose meaning we are looking for. 'If we take all the passages quoted together [Stein says], and moreover remember what was said about original time, no other interpretation remains possible than that by nothingness is meant a being's constitution of being, which is projected with understanding by human beings, i.e. being itself.'[26] Stein compares this distinction between a being's constitution of itself on the one hand and being itself on the

---

24 EES, HA, 'Kant and the Problem of Metaphysics,' pp. 485–6.

25 According to Heidegger's explanations 'what is understood by nothingness is not absolutely nothing. As there is talk of various forms of nothingness and these are not further explained, it remains unclear what kind of nothingness was meant'. EES, HA, 'Kant and the Problem of Metaphysics', p. 491.

26 Ibid.

other with the distinction between essence and existence, which she sees worked out in the *analogia entis*. But Heidegger's reduction of the meaning of being to nothing remains severed from the Scholastic insight that exist-ence is nothing in the sense that it is distinct and different from essence. Stein, in contrast, sympathetic to the idea that being is no thing and also understanding how this nothing could be seen to be the temporalisation inaugurated by the finitude of human experience, cannot extend this same finitude to being as such nor to the meaning of being, as the experience of it includes within it reference to different kinds of being which is not finite in the same way – Infinite Being, which is what it is, i.e. is its own essence, and also essences and essentialities, whose being is not temporal, although they are limited.

Two versions of phenomenology

The alternative proposed by Stein to Heidegger's continuation of phe-nomenology is thus one in which eidetics plays a role complementary to constitutional or transcendental phenomenology, and where analysis of the essence of constituted beings is necessary for the completion of the constitutional analysis. Put in terms closer to Heidegger's: the meaning of being (and of the being of Dasein) cannot be nothing *full stop* and still retain our attention, it must be a fullness in which our desire for meaning can find rest.

We can sketch the difference between Stein and Heidegger's alternative continuations of phenomenology by contrasting ideas of theirs that play comparable roles as well as looking at some shared ideas, which come to play opposite roles. The role of the *eidos* in Stein's version of phenomenology can be seen as parallel to the *existentials* in Heidegger's (a), the function of constitution can be seen as comparable to the idea of projection (b), Stein's understanding of the I, self, soul and person parallels Heidegger's Dasein (c) and her understanding of empathy his *Mitsein* (d). Interpretation, in contrast, bears for both a relationship with values, which is of importance to Heidegger's opposition of authenticity and inauthenticity, and for Stein's opposition of sentient contagion and rationality (e). Death, likewise, and in particular the experience of the death of the other, is understood by the two authors to play opposite roles for the understanding of the meaning of being (f).

Eidos and existentials

Heidegger's existentials – the structures of the being of Dasein – mark the dimensions of Dasein and explain its involvement with the world. They explain the world as much as they explain the being of Dasein, insofar as they constitute the meaning of the world as Dasein opens it up or clears it by or in its being. The existentials – concern, being-in-the-world and being-towards-death – reveal the world in its truth as projected with them and as dependent for its meaning on their projector, Dasein. Existentials structure the world, and it is in this capacity that they play the role played by essence in Stein's view. To Stein essences are understood to be dependent for their translation into mental being on an I. But in themselves their being is essential, *a priori* and not reducible to mental being. What they are constituted *as* can be the object of an eidetic analysis (an analysis of a particular understanding of something), but it remains distinct from an analysis which investigates them as such, i.e. investigates what pertains to them and what does not.[27] Heidegger's existentials, however, although having the same function of being that in terms of which experience is intelligible, cannot really be said to be of a kind of being distinct from that of Dasein. *What* they are is thus neither more nor less difficult to define than Dasein, which we seem to be prohibited from not identifying with nothing.

---

27   Stein's analysis of essence is to be found in Chapter III of *Finite and Eternal Being*.

Constitution and projection

The world is, for Heidegger, dependent on Dasein whether as deteriorated or as authentic. It is projected by Dasein as either by virtue of Dasein's own possibility. The projection is itself projected with the self-initiation that belongs to Dasein in the same way as constitution is itself constituted by the constituting function of the I according to Stein. The constitution of things is consequently dependent on the I in the same way as the world is dependent for its projection on Dasein, but the things themselves, in what they are, i.e. in their essences, are co-constituted by others and *a priori* meaningful. Constitution and projection are according to both authors fundamentally structured by intentionality, but whereas Heidegger's projection emphasises the dependence of the projected on the projector, Stein's constitution emphasises the dependence of constitution on its constituting something objective. To her, only a type of constitution that is infinite can be unlimited by what it constitutes. We can know about such constitution from the possibility of negating the finitude of our own constituting activity, but the fact that we must negate it shows that it is not simply our own.

I, self, soul, person and Dasein

It is the fundamental differentiation between my I and other I's, regarded by Stein as requisite for the inauguration of (human) experience as we know it, which makes me able to access the objectivity of the constituted and puts my ability to access the *a priori* in relief. It is also this differentiation that enables the I to constitute itself as *an* I, one among others, experiencing itself as embodied, and as visible to others as being beings of a certain kind.[28] These embodied, animated beings constitute their world and are

28   Calcagno, *The Philosophy of Edith Stein* is thus right when he writes: 'Our being is constituted in such a way that we are fundamentally related because the very fullness of our person implies the fullness of the other – one cannot fully be without the other' (p. 128). But he is wrong in claiming Stein affirms that 'Each person, besides having his or her own *proprium*, is also a *Mehrheit von Personen*' (ibid.) For Stein a

motivated by it. This means that they constitute values to motivate them, which they might share with others, and which energise them in characteristic ways closed to beings who do not constitute the same values to motivate them. The dimension of openness to the realm of values is according to Stein what makes us constitute human I's as persons. As human personal I's experience themselves as embodied, the feeling of the energy of the values resonating in the psyche opens up a space of depth, which she calls the soul. The constitution of the human person as a personal I having a body and a soul is thus for Stein warranted by experience as we know it. Her account contrasts with Heidegger's account of Dasein, who supposedly does not constitute itself as one of a kind, nor as anything specific at all; in its world projection it is neither a person nor even an I, and it does not have a body or a soul. Such ontic designations would compromise its universality as the meaning of being.

Empathy and Mitsein

As Dasein is not one of a kind, Heidegger's *Mitsein* designates an existential, which structures experience, but it does not open the possibility for another self to make itself manifest as *other* and as *like* me. Nor does *Mitsein* make me constitute myself as an I who is another I for someone else. For Stein, in contrast, empathy enables the I to constitute itself as

---

person is not several – the mistake seems to stem from a mistranslation of a passage concerning *das Man,* which in contrast with the person can refer to a multiplicity of persons. The passage is referred to by Calcagno on p. 118, and he refers to it as MHE 97 – i.e. the old edition of *Martin Heideggers Existentialphilosophie*, from ESW in *Welt und Person* – in the new edition, which we have used, EES p. 469. It reads in our translation: 'If it is recognised that the individual needs the community's support – right from becoming awake to his or her own identity "as such" and "in a specific sense" (i.e. as a member) – and that to a community belong *leading* spirits, who form and determine its lifeforms, then it is no longer possible to see "the they" as a form of deterioration of the self and nothing else. It does not designate a person in the strict sense of the word, but a plurality of persons linked in community who fit themselves into its forms by their Dasein.'

one among many, and it also enables the I to test, confirm and enrich its own perspective by that of the other. *Mitsein* for Heidegger is a semi-inauthentic state of Dasein in which it co-sees the world with others, but not with others who, like it, are themselves Dasein and can correct my worldview by opening a space of objectivity. This air of inauthenticity makes it contrast with Stein's understanding of empathy as an act which is indispensable for the full constitution of the individual I and the person, one's own as well as that of the other, without which authentic objectivity and science is impossible.

Interpretation, authenticity and rationality

The contribution of empathy towards the constitution of individuals whose experience is open to one another enables Stein to conceive of values as motivating objectivities, i.e. as spiritual forces of direction available to all. Values manifest themselves on the one hand in the feelings of the individual human person and on the other as explanatory factors of the emotional life and the character of others, who, like myself, are exposed to their motivating power. Stein understands interpretation as the explanation of the motivation of a text, event, object or institution (itself in turn motivated) in contrast with Heidegger who considers interpretation to be projected by Dasein as its own possibility – the mediation of values being subsumed into Dasein's possibility and hence losing their objectivity and consequent intelligible availability as objective for others, who could also want to realise them. The only measure of the authenticity of the interpretation is, according to Heidegger, whether responsibility for the projection is assumed. To Stein there are other more important criteria: an interpretation has to do justice to what is being interpreted, i.e. account for the motivations that govern it. There is a way to remain below the level of taking responsibility for the interpretation, and that is when opinions are absorbed by sentient contagion and no longer personally tested for their rationality.

Not having an understanding of value-objectivity and its importance for explaining social cohesion, Heidegger will see all collective normativity as an assault on personal independence and an occasion for inauthenticity. *Das Man* is the fallback position of inauthentic Dasein, in which it drowns responsibility in unconscious behaviour. In contrast, Stein maintains the possibility of adequately corresponding to the motivating power of values, and thus being rational, whether or not these values are valued by others.

Death and the meaning of being

For Heidegger death is the end of Dasein, i.e. the end of being-in-the-world (irrespective of the question of a life after death). It is the transition from being Dasein to no longer being Dasein, and it can be undergone only in my own case as Dasein is always mine; but it cannot be experienced as it is the transition from experience to non-experience. In contrast my possibility of not-being is experienced in anguish. An understanding of the totality of Dasein is not advanced by the death of the other and thus the understanding of being cannot be completed, and we cannot advance towards the meaning of being, except provisionally, by existential analysis which in principle cannot be finished except perhaps at our own death. The awareness of the possibility of not-being has nevertheless a sobering effect in that authentic living is being-towards-death in resoluteness or un-guaranteed self-investment, whereas fleeing in front of death leads to inauthentic hiding in 'the they'.

For Stein death is not the proper end of the human being although it is the occasion for its facing finally the question of 'being or not being'. Death can be experienced in my own near-death experiences such as in anguish, severe illness or imminent threat to my life, and it can also be experienced through empathy in the death the other is experiencing, or even from seeing the other already dead. The experience of the different types of death of the other: the fight, the victory and quiet glory shining through, may contribute to our experience of the meaning of being.

The meaning of being cannot for Stein be answered simply by 'Dasein', no matter how well explained it would be in terms of its existentials. Being, for Stein includes different kinds – finite and eternal, personal and non-personal – and reducing being to one of its types is an answer that mistakes a part for the whole. Such a mistake is bound to ignore important features of being as we experience it, first and foremost essence, but also the independent being of natural being, personal individuality, values, community and eternal being.

CHAPTER 12

A Steinian Approach to Dementia

The word *dementia* refers in Latin to the undoing of the mind, to de-minding. In English 'to be demented' still carries the Latin meaning of being out of one's mind, of being mad; someone or something can 'drive you demented' if they are extremely irritating, repetitive, confusing, senseless or silly. Generally however, *dementia* is thought to refer to a spectrum of mental illnesses affecting in particular (but not exclusively) people in old age, illnesses having a physiological substratum responsive to medical treatment, but which are unfortunately not curable at the present time.

Dementia is generally understood to first affect the memory, which Augustine regarded as the place where the soul is rooted in the eternal ideas. In what follows I shall argue, in the light of Stein's phenomenology, that it affects more broadly what she calls 'the function of the I': the ability to *constitute*, to *identify things*, and to *recognise*.[1] When one cannot recognise, one cannot bring the ideas, as Augustine understood them, to bear on past and present experience, and as a consequence one cannot conceptualise and remember. Dementia seems to be experienced by the subject suffering from it as the world becoming increasingly indistinct, confusing and unmanageable. However this does not necessarily mean that the ability to empathise, value and feel is diminished, (except in so far as

---

1 Stein takes the term 'constitution' from Husserl. In PE Chapters 3 and 4 concern 'constitutional issues' (intr. to Chapter 3), in that they concern how the I identifies itself as a psycho-physical individual and a person. Husserl understood constitution as the transcendental function through which an object comes to make sense – he characterised constitution as the 'central viewpoint of phenomenology' (Ideas, § 86).

these presuppose identification).[2] The consequent change in the balance between cognitive and spiritual functions may occasion the development of what could be called a heightened spiritual awareness, since this has to compensate for the intellectual debility acquired. If, as I shall argue, the experience of the 'dark night of the soul' can be helpful for understanding the experience of the person suffering from dementia, it may also explain why spiritual communication is still possible and may indeed be significantly enhanced and enriched.

Dementia presents a challenge for both primary and secondary sufferers. Both have to deal with the fact that *this could be me*.[3] For the carer: it could be me who had dementia; for the sufferer: it could be me who had the task of looking after a person suffering like me. The challenge is that both parties must accept and understand both roles as they are reflected in the eyes of the other; but when it is met, dementia opens the possibility of communication about the deepest of human realities affecting both parties equally: the soul, the person, the spirit beyond the mind and life after death.[4]

2   That there is more to the I than constitution is an idea we find more developed in
      Stein than in Husserl. She regards the person as the subject of the experience of value
      (motivation) whether in feeling, valuation or action. PE, Chapter IV, 2.
3   *On the Problem of Empathy* is a book about the epistemological condition for inter-
      subjective experience. Empathy is the experiencing of the experience of the other
      (whether or not I quite understand what the other is experiencing). I can thus empa-
      thise without knowing (exactly) what the other is experiencing, but not without
      being *open* to experiencing it.
4   As regards the soul, see PE, Chapter III, 3, as regards the person, PE, Chapter IV. By
      'the spirit beyond the mind' I here mean what motivates in a not readily identifiable
      manner, what moves us before we understand it. By 'life after death' I refer to the
      experience of life beyond one's own mental life. The person who is totally depleted of
      psychic energy often experiences such a state as a kind of death, which, to the person's
      own surprise, is not quite death but contains a still life. It seems to be beyond time,
      and identification of things in successive stages is not of great importance whereas
      human kindness carries a meaningfulness, way beyond what the normally function-
      ing young person usually expects.

The challenge is not, however, easily accepted by either of the parties involved.

1. It is not easily accepted that dementia is a human possibility and hence that I also could get dementia. When it is not accepted by the carer, the evasion is experienced by the primary sufferer as an avoidance of the recognition due to him or her, an avoidance which he or she may well understand. This understanding, however, may well be associated with grief for the loss of a relation to the one who no longer recognises, a grief so deep that it may produce either a rejection of one's own experience (because it cannot be experienced by the other) and/or a deepening of love issuing in a waiting for the other until the other is ready to recognise.

2. Seen from the opposite point of view it is not easy for the dementia sufferer to accept the limitations of the carers, especially because he or she has lost the ability to estimate how much is being done for them and what it 'costs'. Trust must replace the lost overview, otherwise the burden of care will become still greater. This may well be understood by the sufferer, and thus trust can become the sufferer's defence of his or her loved ones. Accepting that such vulnerability cannot ultimately be successfully protected by the loved ones amounts to the acceptance of the possibility of death. The sufferers, i.e. the primary sufferer and the secondary sufferers (the carers), can help each other only by their acceptance, and by waiting for each other to accept *living* with the possibility of death and dementia.

However, when the recognition that 'this could be me' succeeds, the profoundest of shared happiness is possible. To meet the challenge presented to us by dementia we are thus in need of a reflection on who we are so as to enable recognition. To provide this we shall first look at the structure of the human person as proposed by Stein (1). Then, again with Stein's help, we shall look at the act of empathy, in which we are aware of the experience of the other, and thus also of the experience of the one who is suffering from dementia (2). Finally, still under Stein's guidance, we shall compare the one suffering from dementia with the person living through the mystical experience of the 'dark night of the soul', as the latter is described by St John of the Cross and discussed in Stein's final work *The Science of the Cross*.

The Structure of the human person according to Edith Stein

For Stein, the human person does not exist in isolation. It is raised by other human beings, learns to understand who it is with the help of others, lives in constant exchange with others, also in its own thoughts, and can think systematically because it has learned language, which it also has learned from and shares with others of its own kind. We consequently experience from two perspectives, as we experience on the one hand what we experience ourselves personally, and then on the other what we experience others to experience (anger in an angry glance, consideration in a kind gesture). This double experience allows us to talk about what 'we' experience: 'we' went to the cinema; 'we' had a lovely time at the party; 'we' were deeply saddened by the news. We thus exist in community, and our way of understanding the world is through and through influenced by the understanding of others. We can say the world is socially constructed, or as Stein says 'inter-subjectively constituted' in that it matters what others think for what I can think about the world, and conversely that it matters what I think for the understanding of the world others' can have.[5] What we think of the world constitutes a reality which we must all deal with in order to deal with the world as it is. When someone regards me as a traitor it constitutes a reality I have to deal with even if I do not share the view.

The people who we are, who recognise each other as such, live together and constitute a myriad of intricate institutions, groups and patterns. We are characterised each by having an 'I', which forms the centre of a person, in that the 'I' is the pole of experience, of my experience. 'I' learn to constitute myself as a person, i.e. understand myself to be the subject not only of experience, but also of motivation and valuation, just as others are experienced by me to be subjects of their own experience, inclusive of their motivation and valuation.[6] In the process of getting to know who I am, I also

5   PPH, II.
6   PE, III, 5 and IV, 4.

come to identify myself as having a body, which embodies my zero point of orientation and allows me to experience the external world by means of various senses, just as those around me have bodies that are similar to mine (even if those of cats are specifically different, and those of women more similar to mine than those of men).[7] Between the externality of my body and the internality of my 'I', I am aware of an inner 'sphere' in which I am alive with the life of my body, which I can feel to be tired, in pain, at rest, exhausted or vigorous, and which Stein calls the psyche.[8] It is in this sphere that motivations are felt; the psyche is like the sounding board of the spiritual world of values, but it is still, like a musical instrument, a physical medium, under the influence of causality, and hence susceptible to be influenced for example by medication (as well as by the weather, electricity and other physical forces). The psyche is also experienced, however, as pertaining to the psychological 'I', which again is under the influence of the personality of the person who I am. What is felt, the objects of motivation, the values I experience, are experienced, in contrast to the physical world, as beyond the influence of causality, as being distinct precisely by being motivating, not causing.[9] The person knows him- or herself as free, i.e. as capable of motivating himself, of choosing between motivations experienced, of turning his or her attention here or there, in short, as capable of motivation. Being spiritual hence simply means to be motivated, and the spirit as such is motivation.[10] When we say the person is spiritual in essence, we mean it experiences itself as primarily motivated, not caused. The personality consists of the person's habitual value responses, reflecting the character of the person and, in psychical beings, his or her temperament conditioned by talents and handicaps. It is the personality that allows the soul to unfold or deepen, so that a shallow personality, i.e. one who does not access the (spiritual) motivating power of the higher values, leaves the

7   PE, III, 4.
8   PPH, I.
9   Ibid., section III and V.
10 PE, IV, 2: 'motivation is the lawfulness of spiritual life'.

depths of the soul in shadow incapable of finding expression in the person's life. At the opposite end of the spectrum we find the person whose personality, because of its acceding to the motivations stemming from the highest of values, allows for the illumination of the depths of the soul so that it finds expression in the life and acts of the person. We call such a person a real or strong personality, not recognising the same personal distinctness to the superficial person.[11]

People are very different, and it is different what or who different persons consider profound. We are puzzled by each other's sense of profundity and learn from each other, and it is in this way that our experience is challenging to others. We value differently, and as a consequence we draw motivational energy from different values: some appreciate art, others science, some love sport, others videogames. When we suffer, given that suffering drains our mental energy, we look for sources of motivational energy that can help us replenish our energy reservoir: we look for values that are higher than those we have known up to now, which have obviously not been sufficient to power us so that our life feels comfortable. We look to others to see whether they know of such values of higher motivating power which we do not, and we look in particular to those who have suffered as we suffer now to see what they have been able to find. In this way the sufferer strangely leads the way towards the depths because he or she must search for more, whereas the contented one needs nothing further.

The mind which we can lose by becoming demented is not exactly the ability to be motivated, the spiritual capacity to receive energy from the sources of power which the values are. The person suffering from dementia seems to be able to feel, and often deeper than the persons of his or her surroundings. Bouts of extreme anguish or deep contentment in the sun or in response to a smile testify to this. Dementia rather seems to rob the person of the ability to identify in an enduring manner (i.e. *in* time and therefore remember *over* time) what is experienced and to think about it (we cannot think, i.e. reason from one thought to the next,

11   PPH, II, II, § 3, c and §4, d. Einführung, II, b, β.

when we cannot remember and hold on to something we have identified or constituted). The experience itself however, is experienced in so far as the motivating powers motivate without the mediation of constitution. The experience of the self is there too, not as reflection on thoughts, but as a direct experience of the realities of the soul without the interpretation imposed by the superstructure of the mind. Often this awareness is breaking out into expression through the suffering at hand so that states of despair or bliss show on the face and in the entire body posture. The mind which throughout the person's life has been its help to understand and put the world in order now cracks open like a shell to be discarded ('if the grain of wheat does not fall to the ground and dies, it will bear no fruit'), to let the soul shine through in its otherworldly beauty and prepare it for what seems to be a transit – in so far as the soul does not seem to be completely dependent upon this reality of time – through detachment from the body. The soul must part with the mind too in so far as it is depending for its operation on the brain.

The losing of one's mind in dementia thus, on such an account, leaves us to contemplate the soul exposed, reverting back to an original state lying before the superimposition of the personality and the habitual value responses of the person. The person is still living, but only 'out of the depths' and often without words or explanations. The forgetting of past destructive habits often gives the soul a second chance of being itself in its original state, experiencing the world anew as a child. Dementia seems like a rehearsal for death, which lets us, those who are dying and those who are to be left behind for a while, glimpse a life beyond the mind and its dependence on time, which is spiritual and more valuable than anything we can lose. When we can affirm this life in each other by recognising it, the sufferings of the demented person are transfigured, and he or she can be allowed to be the instigator of our common appreciation of that which we hold in common: human dignity. He or she is then allowed to lead us into the mystery where he or she is more at home than we are because of the privilege of suffering.

Empathy: Our experience of the other

We use empathy not only to discover and examine what the other is experiencing but also to establish what is expected of us: as indeed that relies on other people's experience of expectation. We thus use empathy to understand the other's understanding of us: by 'reiterated empathy' we empathise with the other's empathy as regards us, and in this manner we get to understand what he or she thinks of us. Empathy is not *per se* sympathy: by means of empathy I can access the experience of the other even if I do not share his motivations but just understand them as possible. I use empathy, for example, when I attempt to solve a crime mystery: I examine the possible motives which I read through the characters of the persons involved also in their attempt to hide things that might reveal their motives. Empathy is thus not an 'extra' in our lives: it is an essential means of orienting ourselves in the world and of understanding it. It is an act the object of which is the experience of the other, in the same way as perception is the act which has the perceived as its object, or memory the remembered as its object.[12]

I do not always, however, understand what the other is experiencing. In the crime investigation scenario I can see somebody experiencing what looks like remorse, for example, but I cannot see the object of his remorse, nor can I be sure, unless I know the person well, that I don't mistake the expression I take to be remorse for his peculiar way of looking pensive. I can be limited in my ability to empathise on three fronts: 1. I can be limited in my spiritual experience due to my personality structure (if, for example, I deny the possibility of there being anything like remorse, due to a remorse I cannot myself get over). 2. I can be limited in my life experience (of how motivational relationships are in fact built up, e.g. of what in fact can lead to remorse) 3. I can be limited in my knowledge of the physical expression of the spiritual experience in the other (and for example mistake the cat's enlarged pupils as a sign of confidence when in fact it is a sign of fear or the man's frown against the sun for an expression of remorse).

12   PE, II.

In the first instance the limitation of my ability to empathise is due to my own personality structure. In this connection it should be emphasised that being insensitive is not the same as being unable to empathise: the insensitive person overlooks motivations of the other and often do so for particular reasons which can be understood. This may be to solve a crime or promote a career, but the persons thus motivated are capable of doing either of these things only because they are capable of empathising and knowing what is expected of them. Insensitivity is thus a chosen state, it may be a character trait, which can be motivated by the negative value of suffering if one does not want to face it in the other or in oneself. Insensitivity is 'curable' however, i.e. the person 'suffering' from it can stop being insensitive and start experiencing the suffering he or she did not want to face beforehand. Then a personal development is called for and usually follows, which generally speaking is considered as positive by all involved. Insensitivity is very common and is mostly a protective mechanism, but it does have serious consequences for those who are not understood and for the character development of the person opting for it.

In the second instance empathy is restricted by a more genuine lack of personal experience: when nothing like it has been experienced previously by the empathiser, when he or she has nothing to compare to the experience facing him or her. This restriction is linked to the third type of restriction mentioned: that of experience with this particular type of expression. If I have never experienced unreciprocated love, I shall not be able to recognise the signs of that in others at first sight. If I have never experienced a nervous breakdown, I shall not be able to understand or properly imagine what is involved in the experience of that without some introduction. Both of these restrictions, however, do not rely on a chosen refusal and are therefore in principle open to correction by further experience, in contrast with the former type, which is in principle closed to correction until the subject lifts the ban on his own sensitivity.

In the meeting with the person affected by dementia, all of these limitations are at play. We might not understand what is involved in losing one's mind in this manner. We might also not want to know either, and we adopt an insensitive attitude that sometimes encapsulates the entire demented person and thus isolates him or her entirely from our experience by, so to speak, blotting him out. This is for the demented person a source of great distress in so far as he or she is aware of the motives for this insensitivity and regrets being the source of such dissimulated distress in loved ones or relations. The better we can accept the demented person's suffering, and that means accept the suffering as a suffering that in principle is possible for us as well (otherwise I could not empathise with it), the better he or she can accept it as a way forward. This way forward is a way that involves exploring uncharted waters and has value for the entire human community because it is possible for human beings to experience in this way, and because communicating about this type of experience is of relevance to all because of this.

However, we must not underestimate the newness of the experience, and hence that it is not immediately accessible to us without us having experienced something like it. To understand what it feels like to lose one's mind or the ability to identify and recognise requires a transformation 'like' the one undergone by the person directly affected by dementia. The primary sufferer can help us accede to this when we listen to him or her as someone who shows us something of what may come, of who we are, through and beyond death, as someone who can help us to get there ourselves. But it seems clear that we must prepare ourselves for feeling as lost and disorientated as they are in order to understand what it is they are showing us. And such preparation is indeed worthwhile, not just because by means of it we can live in solidarity with the primary sufferer, but also because it is – because of this – the 'normal' development of the soul as it matures and readies itself for a greater degree of understanding of all things human. It is normal that our understanding of the world would be not only stretched, but also broken by life and recast many times as we move through our experience attempting to understand why we are here and what we are supposed to be doing. It is normal for the soul to be affected by the suffering, and thus to live with it in order to obtain through it what Stein calls the 'science of the cross': a new and deeper kind of knowledge.

The 'dark night of the soul'

The passion of Jesus is one of those experiences that are available to us through empathy as we hear about it or read the gospels. His carrying of and dying on the cross – a Roman instrument of torture and social control through shame – represents a way of dying that leaves few people unmoved. For Stein the acceptance of the possibility of such suffering, together with its potentially liberating effect for others, was the occasion to contemplate the effect that the acceptance of this experience could have on the one accepting. She calls it a 'science' because it – beyond the shattering of the easy categories of comfortable living – attains a higher ground, a more secure foothold in understanding how things 'really are'. Thus this science is of a truth that is 'alive and active,' i.e. it transforms the person in possession of it from within, penetrating his or her vision of the world. 'It is buried in the soul like a seed that takes root there and grows making a distinct impression on the soul.'[13] When this soul expresses itself concerning its experience something like a theory of this experience can be constructed. This theory pertains to 'Christian philosophy' in so far as it builds upon the assimilated acceptance of the cross as borne by Jesus Christ.[14] It is science as a particular deepening of the view of the human being allows for a keener observation and a more flexible understanding of the depths and even the root of the soul. Stein portrays the latter in the following manner:

> The thoughts of the heart are the original life of the soul at the ground of her being, at a depth that proceeds all splitting into different faculties and their activity. There the soul lives precisely as she is in herself, beyond all that will be called forth in her through created beings. Although this most interior region is the dwelling of God and the place where the soul is united to God, her own life flows out of here before

---

13   SC, pp. 9–10. ESGA 18, p. 5.
14   Stein confesses her philosophy to be 'Christian' from her twin anthropology onwards (although *Potency and Act* may not fall into this category). Her justification for and discussion of this characterisation can be found in FEB, Chapter I, §4. See Chapter 10.

the life of union begins; and this is so, even in cases where such a union never occurs. For every soul has an inmost region and its being is its life.

But this primary life is not only hidden from other spirits but from the soul herself. This is so for various reasons. Primary life is formless. The thoughts of the heart are absolutely not thoughts in the usual sense of the word; they are not clearly outlined, arranged, and comprehensible constructions of the thinking intellect. They must pass through various formulations before they become such constructions. First, they must rise out of the ground of the heart. Then they arrive at a first threshold, where they become noticeable. This noticing is a far more original manner of being conscious than is perception by the intellect. It too lies before the splitting into faculties and activities. It lacks the clarity of purely sensible perception; on the other hand, it is richer than a bare grasping by the intellect. That which arises is perceived as bearing a stamp of value on the basis of which a decision is made: whether to allow what is rising to come up or not. [...]

At the threshold where the rising movements are perceived, types of recognisable spiritual faculties begin to split off and conceivable structures are formed: to these belong thoughts elaborated by the intellect with their reasonable arrangement (these are interior words for which then, exterior words can be found) movements of the mind and impulses of the will that, as active energies, enter all that is connected with the spiritual life.[15]

The science of the cross allows us, because we are brought there by being brought low, to perceive the root of the soul, where the thoughts of the heart arise, and to notice this arising whether we are demented or not. The science helps us through the idea that recognisability (constitution and identification) is necessary for the life of the spirit in order for us to come out the other side, where suffering can be allowed for and accepted, even when it means losing one's mind. It is as such that the science of the cross is particularly helpful for those who deal with people with cognitive impairment: it allows for a type of communication that does not rely on distinctly formed faculties and their specific functions, but which accedes to the deepest spiritual root of the soul where possibly the last decisive 'choices' regarding its life and afterlife are 'taken', where the drama of the soul's transition to life beyond time in death is played out.

---

15   SC, pp. 157–8. ESGA 18, pp. 131–2 (II, 2, § 3, b, g, 'Das Innerste der Seele und die Gedanken des Herzens').

The fact that the soul is robbed of distinct experience, in senses, memory and intellect is a help to it insofar as the thoughts of the heart are no longer camouflaged, drowned out or disturbed by active constitutional activity. This is what the spiritual director can help the soul who is undergoing the dark night of the soul to realise. He or she recognises the soul's suffering as a sign of its maturation and knows it as the hidden secret of divine love that union can be obtained ultimately only in this way. The dark night of the soul in its various stages as portrayed by St John of the Cross is thus in fact the form the maturing of the soul takes: it corresponds to its deepening, to its accessing its own spiritual depths by means of identification with all things human. Through this process the soul relativises its identification with its physical, psychological or intelligible identity, to rest as spiritual at the point where it will be taken up above itself to at the same time fulfil and lose itself in the eternal life of God. The person suffering from dementia is given the same opportunity as the mystic whether or not such experience was sought after or longed for in whatever form. Like for the mystic, the person with cognitive impairment has no say in the choice of its condition: it is night, it has to be accepted. Raving against the night may be an option in the early stages, but soon such impotence will come that even that is no longer possible. And here lies the opportunity and the possibility of peace beyond what the world can give; peace that is salvific for the one 'suffering' it and for everyone else suffering with the one affected: when the dark night of the soul is lived, whether induced by dementia or actively accepted in prayer, *for us*, or just with surrender, its fruit is understanding and the ability to accompany others on the road towards what the mystical tradition calls 'perfection': Love.

***

The person suffering from dementia can teach us about and lead us into the dark night of the soul. And we can reach him or her much better if we dare to go there on our own accord by letting the message of the cross take root in us like a seed. As this, however, is required for our own 'perfection', our reaching maturity of soul as a person, being challenged to go there by the presence of dementia in a loved one or a person in our care, is a help for us to reach our full potential, to become more fully human. Whichever way we look at it, the suffering induced by dementia, is, in the one suffering from it primarily or in the secondary sufferers, salvific as soon as it is accepted as painfully meaningful: from him or her flow streams of living water.

Conclusion

Stein's work forms a whole in which one can discern a development. The movement from phenomenology to metaphysics already happens from the beginning, just as phenomenology is not at any point definitively abandoned. This introduction could thus have been subtitled *Phenomenology and Metaphysics*, or indeed *Phenomenology and the Meaning of Being*, since it is the meaning of being that is the theme of Stein's metaphysics.

Bibliography

Several good bibliographies exist. Apart from the bibliographies found on the IASPES website and in the *Edith Stein Jahrbuch*, the chronological bibliography by Francesco Alfieri must be mentioned, which has appeared as a special issue of the *Edith Stein Jahrbuch*. This is merely a list of the literature cited in this book.

Works by Stein

Collected Works of Edith Stein (Washington DC: ICS Publications, 1986–).
Edith Stein Gesamtausgabe 1–27 (Freiburg – Basel – Vienna: Herder, 2000–2014).
Edith Steins Werke (Freiburg – Basel – Vienna: Herder, 1977–1999).
'Martin Heidegger's Existential Philosophy', transl. by Mette Lebech in *Maynooth Philosophical Papers*, 2007, Maynooth, pp. 55–98.
Thomas von Aquin Über die Wahrheit, transl. by Edith Stein (Wiesbaden: Marixverlag, 2013 (Kindle)).

Other works

Beckmann, Beate, *Phänomenologie des religiösen Erlebnisses. Religionsphilosophische Überlegungen im Anschluss an Adolph Reinach und Edith Stein* (Würzburg: Königshausen und Neumann, 2003).
Beckmann, and Gerl-Falkovitz, Hanna-Barbara (eds), *Edith Stein. Themen Bezüge Dokumente* (Würzburg: Königshausen und Neumann, 2003).

Beckmann-Zöller, Beate, and Gerl-Falkovitz, Hanna-Barbara (eds), *Die unbekannte Edith Stein: Phänomenologie und Sozialphilosophie* (Frankfurt am Main: Peter Lang, 2006).

Betschart, Christof, 'Was ist Lebenskraft? Edith Steins erkenntnistheoretischen Prämissen in "Psychische Kausalität" (Teil 1)' in *Edith Stein Jahrbuch* 2009, pp. 154–84.

Betschart, Christof, 'Was ist Lebenskraft? Edith Steins anthropologischer Beitrag in "Psychische Kausalität" (Teil 2)' in *Edith Stein Jahrbuch* 2010, pp. 33–64.

Borden Sharkey, Sarah, *Thine Own Self. Individuality in Edith Stein's Later Writings* (Washington DC: The University of America Press, 2010).

Calcagno, Antonio, *The Philosophy of Edith Stein* (Pittsburgh: Duquesne University Press, 2007).

Conrad-Martius, Hedwig, 'Zur Ontologie und Erscheinungslehre der realen Außenwelt. Verbunden mit einer Kritik positivistischer Theorien', in *Jahrbuch für Philosophie und Phänomenologische Forschung* 3, 1916, pp. 345–542.

Conrad-Martius, Hedwig, *Metaphysische Gespräche* (Halle: Niemeyer, 1921).

Conrad-Martius, Hedwig, 'Realontologie', in *Jahrbuch für Philosophie und Phänomenologische Forschung*, 6, 1923, pp. 159–333.

Conrad-Martius, Hedwig, *Das Sein* (Munich: Kosel Verlag, 1957).

Denziger, H., and Bannwart, C., *Enchiridion Symbolorum, definitionum et declarationum de rebus fidei et morum* (1928 edition).

Drummond, John (ed.), *Phenomenological Approaches to Moral Philosophy. A Handbook* (Dordrecht: Kluwer, 2002).

Etlinger, Max, *Beiträge zur Lehre von der Tierseele und ihrer Entwicklung* (Münster: Aschendorf, 1925).

Gadamer, Hans Georg, *Truth and Method*, trans. ed. by Garrett Barden and John Cumming (London: Sheed and Ward, 1975).

Gurmin, Haydn, and Lebech, Mette, *Phenomenology, Humanity, Being. Proceedings of the first IASPES conference* (Nordhausen: Traugott Bautz, forthcoming).

Habermas, Jürgen, *The Inclusion of the Other*, ed. by Ciaran Cronin and Pablo DeGreif (Cambridge: Polity Press, 2002).

Hering, Jean, 'Bemerkungen über das Wesen, die Wesenheit und die Idee', in *Jahrbuch für Philosophie und phänomenologische Forschung*, 1921, pp. 495–543.

Herbstrith, Waltraud, *Edith Stein. A Biography*, transl. by Fr. Bernhard Bonowitz, O.C.S.O (San Francisco: Ignatius Press, 1992).

Husserl, Edmund, *Vorlesungen über Ethik und Wertlehre*, Husserliana Bd. XXVIII.

Husserl, Edmund: *Logical Investigations* 1–2, transl. by J.N. Findlay (London–New York: Routledge, 2001).

Husserl, Edmund, *Ideas pertaining to a pure Phenomenology and to a phenomenological Philosophy. First Book,* transl. by F. Kersten (Dordrecht: Kluwer, 1983).

Husserl, Edmund, *Ideas pertaining to a pure Phenomenology and to a phenomenological Philosophy. Second Book,* transl. by R. Rojcewicz and A. Schuwer (Dordrecht: Kluwer, 1989).

Huth, Albert, *Pädagogische Anthropologie* (Leipzig: Klinckhardt, 1932).

Ingarden, Roman, 'Essentiale Fragen. Ein Beitrag zum Wesensproblem', in *Jahrbuch für Philosophie und Phanomenologishe Forschung*, 5, 1925, pp. 125 ff.

Jani, Anna, 'Von der Welterfahrung zur geistigen Welt. Spuren der Dilthey-Rezeption in Edith Steins frühen Schriften' forthcoming in *Edith Stein Jahrbuch* 2015.

Lebech, Mette, 'Study-guide to Edith Stein's *Philosophy of Psychology and the Humanities*' in *Yearbook of the Irish Philosophical Society*, 2004, ed. by Mette Lebech, pp. 40–76.

Lebech, Mette, *On the Problem of Human Dignity. A Hermeneutical and Phenomenological Investigation* (Würzburg: Königshausen und Neumann, 2006).

Lebech, Mette, 'Why do we need the Philosophy of Edith Stein?' in *Communio International Catholic Review*, Winter 2011, XXXVIII, no. 4, pp. 682–727.

Lukas, Andreas, 'Recht und Staat bei Edith Stein' in *Edith Stein Jahrbuch* 2014, pp. 92–110.

MacIntyre, Alisdair, *Edith Stein. A Philosophical Prologue 1913–1922* (New York – Toronto – Oxford: Rowman and Littlefield Publishers, 2006).

Neubach, Helmut, *Kleine Geschichte Schlesiens* (Görlitz: Senfkorn, 2007).

Nota, John, 'Edith Stein and Martin Heidegger', in *Carmelite Studies 4, Edith Stein Symposium*, ed. John Sullivan (Washington DC: ICS Publications, 1987) pp. 50–73.

Ott, Hugo, 'Edith Stein und Freiburg', in *Studien zur Philosophie von Edith Stein* (Freiburg – Munich: Verlag Karl Alber, 1993), pp. 107–45.

Parsons, Judith, *Edith Stein: Toward an Ethic of Relationship and Responsibility*, Duquesne University 2005 (doctoral dissertation).

Pfeiffer, Alexandra, *Hedwig Conrad-Martius. Eine Phänomenologische Sicht auf Natur und Welt* (Würzburg: Königshausen und Neumann, 2005).

Przywara, Erich, 'Edith Stein. Zu ihrem zehnten Todestag', in *In und Gegen* (Nuremberg: Glock und Lutz, 1955).

Reinach, Adolph, 'Concerning Phenomenology', trans. Dallas Willard, *The Personalist* 50 (1969), pp. 194–221, reprinted in *The Phenomenology Reader*, ed. D. Moran and T. Mooney (London and New York: Routledge, 2002) pp. 180–96.

Reinach, Adolph, 'Die Überlegung: ihre ethische und rechtliche Bedeutung', *Gesammelte Schriften*, pp. 121–65 and *Sämtliche Werke,* pp. 279–311.

Ripamonti, Lidia, 'Being Thrown or Being held in Existence? The opposite Approaches to Finitude of Edith Stein and Martin Heidegger', in *Yearbook of the Irish Philosophical Society* 2008, ed. Fiachra Long, pp. 71–83.

Sawicki, Marianne, *Body Text and Science. The Literacy of Investigative Practices and the Phenomenology of Edith Stein* (Dordrecht: Kluwer, 1997).

Sawicki, Marianne, 'Making up Husserl's Mind about Constitution', in *Yearbook of the Irish Philosophical Society* 2007, ed. Will Desmond, pp. 191–216.

Scheler, Max, *Formalism in Ethics and Non-Formal Ethics of Values*, transl. by Frings and Funk (Evanston: Northwestern University Press, 1973).

Scheler, Max, *The Nature of Sympathy* (London: Routledge and Keegan Paul, 1954).

Scheler, Max, *Ressentiment*, transl. by William W. Holdheim (New York: Schocken, 1972).

Smith, James H., *Wert, Rechtheit and Gut. Adolph Reinach's Contribution to Early Phenomenological Ethics*. Doctoral dissertation, National University of Ireland, Maynooth (now Maynooth University), 2013.

Tönnies, Ferdinand, *Community and Society*, trans. and ed. by Charles P. Loomis (New York: Harper and Row, 1963).

Index of Names

Index of Terms

Lightning Source UK Ltd.
Milton Keynes UK
UKHW021816180722
406016UK00007B/1565